FAITH

Whot It Is and What It Isn't

FAITH
What It Is and What It Isn't

Terrence W. Tilley

ORBIS BOOKS

Maryknoll, New York 10545

Founded in 1970, Orbis Books endeavors to publish works that enlighten the mind, nourish the spirit, and challenge the conscience. The publishing arm of the Maryknoll Fathers and Brothers, Orbis seeks to explore the global dimensions of the Christian faith and mission, to invite dialogue with diverse cultures and religious traditions, and to serve the cause of reconciliation and peace. The books published reflect the views of their authors and do not represent the official position of the Maryknoll Society. To learn more about Maryknoll and Orbis Books, please visit our website at www.maryknollsociety.org.

Published by Orbis Books, Maryknoll, New York 10545–0302.
Manufactured in the United States of America.
Manuscript editing and typesetting by Joan Weber Laflamme.

Queries regarding rights and permissions should be addressed to: Orbis Books, P.O. Box 302, Maryknoll, New York 10545–0302.

Library of Congress Cataloging-in-Publication Data

Tilley, Terrence W.
      Faith : what it is and what it isn't / Terrence W. Tilley.
        p. cm.
      Includes bibliographical references (p.) and index.
      ISBN 978-1-57075-879-9 (pbk.)
  1. Faith. I. Title.
      BT55.T48 2010
      210—dc22

                                               2010002399

Contents

Acknowledgments

My indebtedness to the works of Paul Tillich *(Dynamics of Faith),* H. Richard Niebuhr *(Radical Monotheism and Western Culture),* and to my teacher, James Wm. McClendon, Jr., should be obvious. My other intellectual debts are captured in the references and works consulted and in the acknowledgments in my own earlier works, upon which I occasionally drew in composing this book.

Dermot Lane and Phyllis Zagano have read and helpfully commented on some of the chapters. Maureen Tilley, Michael Barnes, and Jeffrey Coleman, my graduate assistant in fall 2009, read the entire text and made numerous contributions to improving the style, arrangement, and logic of the argument. Barbara Hilkert Andolsen, Erica Olson, and Catherine Osborne used the first two chapters with students in the required frosh theology course at Fordham, "Faith and Critical Reasoning," and provided a number of insights that helped clarify the writing. My own first-year seminar students endured the entire text and through their responses made this a more readable book. Thanks go to them: Teddy Allen, Isabel Arissó, Claire Dugan, Nicole Casey, Courtney Congjuico, Megan Cookson, Holly Curtis, Lauren Duca, Danielle Eaton, Jessica Frasier, Bryan Healy, Genevieve Looby, Brendan Malone, Caitlin Kelly Nosal, Rachel Pincus, Melissa Neri, Eva Raimondi, Gabrielle Richter, and Kaitlin Shortell. Susan Perry, the patient editor at Orbis Books who shepherded this text to completion, has helped on numerous occasions.

With all these debts, one would think there would be no mistakes left in the text! But I suspect there are errors and infelicities, and for them the author alone is responsible.

Introduction

As we enter the second decade of the twenty-first century, understanding the concept of faith has become increasingly important, yet increasingly difficult. Important because faith is a powerful human reality all too often ignored or misunderstood in our public discourse. Difficult because students and scholars, pundits and politicians talk a lot about faith yet fail to recognize the fundamental importance of faith in the lives of individuals and societies.

The importance of seeking to understand the currents of faith was underlined by the late writer David Foster Wallace. The Kenyon College commencement ceremony in 2005 heard his version of this old story:

> There are these two young fish swimming along and they happen to meet an older fish swimming the other way, who nods at them and says "Morning, boys. How's the water?" And the two young fish swim on for a bit, and then eventually one of them looks over at the other and goes "What the hell is water?"

Wallace deftly portrayed our situation with regard to faith. We are awash in seas of faith. Yet we often fail to recognize that each of us has a faith and that faith shapes all of our lives. We think that some of us live "without faith"; but, as we shall see, a human without faith is like a fish out of water.

Wallace reminded the class of 2005 that higher education should enable people to think and live better, not just to get a better job. He showed how important it is to understand how our faith shapes our minds and hearts, our actions and relationships. In our increasing concern with developing "marketable skills" in our colleges and universities, even educated people may be like the young fish. Although we swim in seas of faith, we don't recognize how the currents of faith shape the course of our life. We do not even know how to ask "how's the faith" because we can't answer the question "what the hell is faith?"

We cannot say what faith is because we also fail to recognize the gods that command our devotion. Most Americans claim to believe in God. Yet many of us spend one hour most weeks with God and the other 167 hours with other objects of our devotion—money, power, knowledge, prestige, and so forth. The point is not to decry such "idolatry." The point is to recognize both what gods we actually have faith in and how that faith shapes our lives.

Many people seem to reduce the multifaceted reality of faith to only one of its dimensions. Hence, Chapter 1 addresses the common misunderstandings of faith. Chapter 2 explores what faith is: a relationship to the gods or God that gives our lives meaning. We will see that even those who have no religious faith nonetheless have their own faiths. And, as we shall see, even atheists worship their own sorts of gods. Chapters 3 and 4 explore the expressions of faith using a variety of creeds, stories, symbols, and practices drawn from a variety of faith traditions. But we live in a world with multiple faith traditions. Thus, Chapter 5 offers criteria for evaluating faith in a world in which faiths are in serious, even deadly, conflict. Because evaluating faith is a personal task, applying the criteria necessarily is left to you, if you wish to take it up.

We may be blind to the power of the faith that shapes our lives. This book is an exercise in learning how to see our faiths clearly so we can figure out how we can live well together in a world in which faith both unites and divides us.

1

Misunderstanding Faith

Faith is one of the most misunderstood words in the English language. To display what faith is, we begin by understanding these misunderstandings. Beginning with these confusions paves the way to showing a more adequate understanding of faith.

Four kinds of misunderstanding of faith are common. The first reduces faith to believing things. The second equates having faith with behaving morally. The third reduces faith to something that we feel "deep in our souls." The fourth misunderstanding equates having faith with being religious.

Each misunderstanding contains an important, but partial, insight about faith. If you now accept only a "partial truth" about the concept of faith, this exercise should lead you to a better understanding of what faith is.

FAITH AND BELIEF

The *rationalist* misunderstanding of faith is very common. This view mistakenly equates faith with *believing* a proposition or claim, for example, "God created and sustains the universe." This misunderstanding can be found among both skeptics and believers.

Skeptical Rationalism

Mark Twain once put the skeptical position most aptly: "Faith is believing what you know ain't so." The skeptical rationalist sees faith as the enemy of reason and reasonableness. People of faith are unreasonable—at least with regard to what they believe on faith. Or so the hard core skeptics like Twain think. Skeptics find that persons of faith believe a proposition that makes a factual claim on the basis of little or no evidence or argument. "They take it 'on faith' (and are fools to do so)" expresses this skeptical viewpoint.

Of course, skeptics like Twain are right about something: "Blind faith" is indeed an enemy of reason. But faith is never entirely blind. Typically, people accept claims "on faith" from people they have reason to trust.

The root of this misunderstanding is equating faith with having a belief or a particular set of beliefs. The insight of this view is that belief is a *component* of faith. The confusion of this view is thinking that faith is *identical* to belief.

To believe people in authority can be perfectly reasonable. We take things "on faith" from our teachers, our parents, and even our political leaders. When my physicist colleague tells me that she can prove "$E=mc^2$," I have to take it "on faith" that she can do so and that the claim is true. I would not know the difference between a valid proof of that equation and a pile of mathematical gibberish. I am not a physicist. But that doesn't mean I have *blind* faith in my colleague in physics. Rather, I know that those who are "in the know"—the community of physicists—can tell the difference. And unless she was lying or fooling around, my "faith" in what she says is really based in my trust in her both as my colleague and as a competent physicist. My trust in her is not blind, but informed, at least minimally.

Some people indeed do seem to have blind faith, at least sometimes. In 2003, President George W. Bush insisted that the people of the United States should support his policy of invading Iraq. He claimed that Iraq's leader, Saddam Hussein, had hidden stockpiles of weapons of mass destruction. Although little or no evidence was given for this claim—and it was later shown to be dubious, at best—President Bush more or less asked the Congress and the American people to take it "on faith" that such weapons existed. When no weapons were found, the Congress and the people had their trust in him undermined. When we discover our trust has been misplaced, we lose our trust in the person we trusted because we realize that we were betrayed by someone who abused our faith.

The difference between my trust in my colleague and my trust in the president is crucial. The difference is not that I agreed with one and disagreed with the other—I didn't know enough really to agree *or* disagree with them. The issue is this: her claim had independent support. The president's did not.

In fact, one of the hallmarks of the scientific method is that scientific claims are accepted *if and only if* another scientist can independently reproduce the experiment or analysis that warrants the claim. For example, the 1989 proposal of "cold fusion"—that nuclear fusion could take place at temperatures far lower than the temperature at which nuclear fusion "ordinarily" occurs—created a great stir. But when other scientists could not replicate the results and found errors in the experiment that led to claims about the possibility of cold fusion, the claim was discredited.

The conditions of secrecy that President Bush imposed made any independent checking of his administration's claim by competent and independent investigators impossible. Weapons inspectors from the United Nations had searched for years without finding any evidence for Iraq's having weapons of mass destruction. Admittedly, Iraq's leader, Saddam Hussein, had stonewalled the search frequently, but he never brought it to a halt. Rather than allowing the inspectors to continue to search, beginning the war made independent verification not merely difficult, but impossible. In effect, President Bush not only demanded that the Congress and the nation trust him blindly but also seemed to ensure that the trust would remain "blind."

Of course, one may accept a particular claim "on faith," and that claim may well be true. Those who get us to accept that claim may indeed be telling us what is true. Even blind faith is not *necessarily* deceptive. Nor does blind faith *necessarily* lead one to error. But blind faith or blind trust is a con artist's stock in trade. Blind trust makes one vulnerable to being deceived by those who claim they know something but offer no evidence. Blind faith accepts claims—whether true or false—without recourse to reason. The skeptic's insight is correct: blind faith is finally irrational.

But not all trust or faith is blind. Another insight we can draw from the skeptic's criticism is that one's faith can never be conclusively verified or falsified in the ways scientific claims can. We cannot have absolute certainty in faith. The beliefs a person holds on faith only rarely can be conclusively shown true or false. This does not make all faith irrational. Rather, it shows that real faith is a risk—one that one should take with one's eyes wide open, not blindly.

The Risk of Faith

The classic expression of the risk of faith is Pascal's Wager. Blaise Pascal (1623–62) was a committed Roman Catholic. He argued roughly as follows: Either God exists or God does not exist. If God exists and one lives a life faithful to God, one's gain is infinite: eternal life in heaven. If God does not exist, and one lives a life faithful to God, one's loss is finite: some temporary joys and pleasures on this earth. If God does not exist, and one lives a life free from religious strictures, one's gain is finite: some temporary joys and pleasures on this earth. If God exists, and one does not live a faithful life, one incurs an infinite loss: the loss of the eternal love of God. Given finite loss or gain versus infinite loss or gain, one ought to wager on God's existence because that is the only wager that has the possibility of gaining an infinite benefit at finite cost. The cost of the other wagers is finite, and the benefits of the other wagers are finite at best, infinitely negative at worst. Therefore, the wise bet—the one with least to lose and the most to gain—is to wager one's life on God.

Few today think such a wager is either convincing or valid. Pascal evidently assumed that the only real god is God (that is, "god" with a lower case "g" is a common noun, but "God" with an upper case "G" designates the god of Judaism, Christianity, and Islam—Chapter 2 will spell out the importance of recognizing this difference). Assuming God is the only god cannot be taken for granted. There are many possible gods. The ancient Greeks and Romans had many gods. On which should one wager? One of theirs? Some other god? Why only gods who might seem infinite? Also, the possibility of measuring finite versus infinite seems impossible. How can one compare what is "not finite" to what is "finite"? We know how to compare oranges and apples with regard to their sweetness or color, but how can we possibly compare something finite (bounded, limited) to something infinite (unbounded, unlimited)?

Over the centuries, philosophical debate has raged over what the Wager argument was and what it meant (the interpretation here is merely one of many). Some even find it a prime example of a misunderstanding of faith, the voluntarist misunderstanding discussed later in this chapter. So what good *is* such a disputable and dubious argument?

The Wager argument underlines the fact that faith—whatever faith one has—is a risk. There is no apodictic certainty in matters of faith. And what each of us risks is our life. In the early days of network television, the comedian Groucho Marx hosted a quiz show called "You Bet Your Life!" Exactly. Faith involves a bet or a risk one takes—whatever one's faith, one bets one's life.

Now someone might say that we should avoid having faith, avoid the risk of faith. However, Pascal's Wager shows that even the person without faith in God or (seemingly) any god has values. One without religious faith may most highly value money, fame, power, success, one's family, or one's nation. The Wager shows that whatever finite good one most highly values is uncertain. Our wealth may crash in a depression, our fame may be fleeting, our power overpowered, or our success undermined by bad luck or even our enemies. The Wager reminds us that we live *for* something. Hence, no life is without risk because what we *do* live for may not *be* worth betting our life on.

We may try to gain certainty in belief by relying on an inspired book. But *which* book? Why prefer the Hebrew Bible over the Christian Bible or the Qur'an or the Buddhist Tripitika or other sacred texts? The answer that some religious people give is, "Because God inspired (or revealed) the book." But that misses the point. The point is to acquire certainty about the reality of a god who allegedly revealed or inspired the text.

However, one cannot gain certainty about which god—if any—exists by assuming that a particular sacred text was revealed by that god. Such reasoning is so viciously circular that it borders on self-deception. Such reasoning is like having a card in one's hand that on one side says, "The Bible is true because God revealed it; for proof, see other side," and on the other says, "God is real because the Bible tells me so; for proof, see other side." The same argument applies to proving the reality of YHWH from the Hebrew Bible, the Trinity from the Christian Bible, or Allah from the Qur'an. Such "arguments" are, bluntly, worthless to give certainty to one's faith.

In short, in a world with multiple faith traditions, including traditions like scientific materialism, secular humanism, and various forms of atheism that seem to reject any and all gods, we cannot avoid this fact: life is a risk. No matter what we most highly value, we may be wrong. "You Bet Your Life!" tells a profound truth. No faith I know of is *perfectly* reasonable and without risk.

Believing Rationalism

A believing rationalism is the mirror image of the *skeptical rationalist* misunderstanding. Whereas the skeptic construes faith as irrational belief that a proposition is true, the believing rationalist view reduces faith to one's acceptance of some propositions as true. These propositions are the foundations of faith—hence, this can be called a *foundationalist* approach.

Some foundationalists find that one has to take those propositions "on faith" or on the basis of a sacred text (even if those texts cannot provide absolute certainty). These foundationalists are fideists (from the Latin, *fides*, "faith"). Others believe that there are good arguments to support the rationality of accepting foundational propositions like "God exists." Once one is convinced of the truth of these propositions, one has the basic beliefs on which a system of religious thought can be developed. These foundationalists are rationalists.

Fideists exhort one to accept basic propositions on faith. One then bases one's reasoning on these propositions. They are true because God has revealed them through an inspired prophet or a revealed text. These beliefs are neither to be doubted nor investigated, but rather accepted on faith. One accepts the revelation on faith because God can neither deceive nor be deceived. But even if God is trustworthy to reveal what is true in general, how can we discern which propositions are revealed in particular? The question noted above returns: Why accept the Hebrew Bible over the Christian Bible or either over the Qur'an? Why is the choice not arbitrary?

Some philosophers are *rational foundationalists*. They believe that one can show through argument the reasonableness of accepting a proposition, such as "God exists," as the ultimate basis of faith. If one can show that it is rational to accept such propositions, one has shown that the faith founded on those propositions is reasonable. I have no general quarrel with such philosophical arguments. Each argument needs to be evaluated on its own terms. Some are more convincing than others. However, these arguments typically show that accepting a proposition like "God exists" is *as reasonable as* accepting other propositions, such as "only the universe that science shows us exists." They do not succeed in showing that "God exists" is the *only* or the *most* reasonable proposition one can have about the ultimate cause and destiny of the universe, just that it is *a* reasonable proposition to believe. Hence, even a successful discovery of a rational foundation for faith does not remove the risk of faith.

Some philosophers do argue for basic beliefs as a component of faith. They do not assume that having faith is accepting propositions. They simply argue that a reasonable person can accept a proposition such as "God exists" and that this reasonableness is a foundation for her or his faith. These philosophers typically attempt to rebut those skeptical rationalists who attack a faith claim as unreasonable or blind. These philosophers do not misunderstand faith but focus on one aspect of faith in their work in responding to challenges. However, another more common mistake is found when one equates faith with belief.

The Gallup Fallacy

One common form of the rationalist misunderstanding can be called the Gallup fallacy. Public opinion polls show that a vast majority of U.S. citizens, typically over 90 percent, believe in God or a universal spirit and that 80 percent believe in heaven.

The results of any poll, of course, can be skewed by the way one asks the questions. But assuming that such polls are roughly accurate, what does this poll tell us about the faith of the majority of the citizens of the United States? Almost nothing.

The acceptance of a proposition alone does not correlate with one's faith. To say that Catholics, Muslims, Jews, most vaguely religious people, and many who claim to be "spiritual, but not religious"—almost all of whom would assent to the proposition that there is a God or universal spirit—have "the same faith" would be ludicrous. Even if public opinion polls are fair and accurate, we commit a Gallup fallacy if we infer that such acceptance of a proposition says much about a person's or a nation's faith.

The root of the Gallup fallacy is assuming that having faith is the same thing as believing a proposition. It takes having faith as equivalent to the acceptance of a proposition. This equation is an error. Rather, the insight we can glean here is that propositions that express our beliefs are a *component* of our faith.

The attempt to remove the risk involved in a life of faith by showing a proposition like "God exists" to be reasonable is a failure. It may be not unreasonable to believe in God—or in the dharma or the Tao—but whether one lives out a faith that is in accord with the Bible, the Qur'an, the Tao Te Ching, or the findings of science is another matter entirely.

In sum, faith and reason are neither antithetical nor identical. Faith always involves risk. Blind faith is an irrational risk. Since beliefs or propositions are not the equivalent of faith, but only a component of faith, proving a proposition does not make a faith claim perfectly rational. There is a difference between accepting a proposition, even a certain one, and having faith. But how we reason about and in faith is material for the rest of the book.

FAITH AND MORALITY

Most days as I leave work to catch the bus home, a street preacher bellows across the street from the bus stop. The substance of his message each day is basically the same: The world's morality is going to hell in a handbasket (the topics change from day to day—most of the immorality is, of course, sexual). If you accept the world's morality, you are going to hell. To avoid the eternal punishment consequent on living an immoral life, "turn away from the world's lure and turn to Jesus by accepting him as your personal Lord and Savior."

Although the preacher's approach is simpler, he has inherited a view that was very strong in nineteenth-century literature. In Fyodor Dostoevsky's great novel *The Brothers Karamazov*, the character Ivan Karamazov thought that without God everything is lawful. In Matthew Arnold's *Literature and Dogma*, religion is defined as "morality touched by emotion." When the Roman Catholic (First) Vatican Council named "faith and morals" as the topics on which the pope of the Roman Catholic Church might exercise infallibility, it assumed the linkage. Clearly, our street preacher's proclamations have been informed, however distantly, by this nineteenth-century concept that having faith means living morally. Faith is seen as intrinsically connected with morality, or as the (only) root of morality.

That there is a connection between one's faith and one's actions seems obvious. If I say I have faith in Allah, and yet enjoy pork and port, one may wonder what sort of faith I have, whether my saying I am a Muslim is just a sham. If I am a Roman Catholic, I may differ strongly with one or more of my fellow Catholics about the fundamental morality of free-market capitalism. Yet we typically see our shared Catholic faith as normatively shaping our moral views—each just thinks the other is mistaken. If my actions or practices do not in some way fit my profession of faith, they may show my faith to be the faith of a hypocrite.

The ordinary connection of forms of religion with moral practices is shown by the oddness of some phrases that combine faith with practices: "Buddhist butcher," "Methodist wine expert," "Baptist bootlegger." There may be actual people these phrases describe. Yet these are odd phrases, oxymorons. Their oddity is connecting a specific faith tradition with a specific practice that does not really fit with the behavior ordinarily expected of a member of that faith tradition. These oxymorons show that some patterns of conduct are not appropriate for members of specific religious faith traditions. One's faith is or should ordinarily be connected to one's moral choices and practices, encouraging some choices, discouraging others.

There *is* a connection between faith and morality. The problem is seeing clearly just what the connection is.

The Moralists' Error

Equating faith to morality is confused in a very particular way; this is the *moralist* misunderstanding of faith. Morality has to do with acts of will, with choices. Faith may shape our choices, but it is not identical to them. Our faith is not merely morality, even though there are usually *links* between faith and morals. That was the insight of the nineteenth-century writers noted above. It is a confusion to *equate* the two.

Our moral *choices* are voluntary—if they are involuntary we are not morally responsible for them. My choice to have a dry martini is voluntary. It may be an amoral, immoral, or moral choice, depending on a host of circumstances. If I am an alcoholic, one might think that my choice to drink is not voluntary. Of course, the disease or vice of alcoholism disposes me to drink. But that vice or disposition does not *force* me to walk into a bar and order a martini or into a liquor store to buy a bottle of gin.

My choice to go to church is voluntary. If I am a person of the Catholic faith, one might think that my choice to go to a Catholic church on some Sunday is not voluntary. Admittedly, my faith commitment may dispose me to go to church, but it does not force me to do so. I still have a choice in the matter.

Yet if I never went to church or went out of my way to avoid going to church, such a pattern of behavior would raise questions about my faith. Am I a hypocrite? Is my alleged Catholicism really a sham? At least, I would have to be able to explain *why* my odd behavior is compatible with my faith.

Indeed, people have debated extensively about whether particular actions or attitudes are compatible with a particular faith. Can I drink alcohol if I am a Methodist? (Some say no, but others are more lenient.) Can I dance or play cards on the Sabbath if I am a Southern Baptist? (The answer depends a lot on what kind of Baptist one is.) Can married Roman Catholics use contraceptives to limit the number of babies they have? (The teaching authority of the Catholic Church says no, but a vast majority of Roman Catholics say yes.) The understanding of which acts are compatible with a faith tradition is not simple but complex; it is not static but may change over time; it is not universal but may shift with race, ethnicity, gender, class, or other factors.

Our *dispositions* include our tendencies to make certain choices rather than others. We can have dispositions or tendencies that we rarely, if ever, act on. Our moral dispositions are our tendencies to make certain choices rather than others. Our faith may dispose us to make certain choices rather than others, and thus function as one of our moral dispositions. But our faith is identical with neither our choices nor our dispositions.

Our dispositions lie at the heart of our morality. Yet how our dispositions are linked to our values, our choices, and our practices is sometimes hard to discern. Twice during my eleven-year career as a nursing orderly in a hospital, I ran into patients' rooms where fires had broken out to try to rescue them. At no other time when I was on duty did a fire break out in our hospital. But when they did occur, that's how I reacted. I certainly do not make a habit of running into smoke-filled rooms. But do I have a disposition to rush in to help in emergency situations? Perhaps. But what is the root of that disposition? Is it rooted in my faith? My upbringing? Bluntly, I have no idea—and that is, I believe, because the relationship between a person's disposition and its roots is truly murky. Even if one's faith seems to dispose one to engage in certain forms of behavior and avoid others, being sure that faith is a root of a disposition may be impossible. This uncertainty suggests that it is unwarranted to identify faith as the same thing as a disposition to act in certain ways.

Our virtues and vices are our moral practices, the enduring patterns of action rooted in our moral dispositions, expressive of our values, and displayed in our choices. Philosophers have discussed the range of virtues and vices since antiquity. The cardinal virtues—prudence, fortitude, temperance, and justice—are found on almost every list. The list of vices seems more varied; one list names the "seven deadly sins" of lust, gluttony, greed, sloth, wrath, envy, and pride. Many of us are well acquainted with at least some of them.

One of my vices is impatience—I have a tendency to be irritable and frustrated in certain circumstances. I snap at machines that fail to function and people who fail to do tasks that need to get done in a timely manner so I can do my own work on time. Like most people aware that they have a vice, I work on ways to overcome that vice—in my case, striving to be more patient.

The point is that there is not a one-to-one relationship between faith and morality. Nor is my faith a result of my moral choices touched with emotion. It is an error to equate faith with morality—whether we understand morality as fundamentally disposition or choice or act of will or habit—or even morality tinged with emotion. The insight at the root of this misunderstanding, of course, is that one's faith *affects* one's moral dispositions, choices, and habits, even though faith is not the only factor that affects one's morality and in some instances may have little effect on one's morality. Reducing faith to morality or morality to faith is a confusion.

Faith and the Will

The nineteenth-century link between faith and morals noted above is also found in the work of the American pragmatist philosopher William James. James especially seemed to equate faith with the will in his famous essay "The Will to Believe." He argued—against the rationalists of his own day—that in a particular situation, a "genuine option situation," one had a right to believe a claim for which one had insufficient evidence. If one were in a situation that was forced (between mutually exclusive options), living (so that the available options were at least somewhat appealing), momentous (so that if one did not choose *now*, one would lose the possibility of taking any of the options), and not decidable on the basis of evidence available, then one could "will to believe" as one wished. James successfully showed that in a "genuine option situation," one had no choice but to choose, even though one could not make a choice determined by *rational* means.

Imagine that you are driving to an airport, rushing to catch a flight you cannot miss no matter what. You approach a junction;

there are two freeways you could take. Sometimes one is quicker, sometimes the other. You don't know how the traffic is moving on either today. You have to catch your plane. Your situation is forced (no other route available), living (both routes have worked in the past), momentous (if you take the wrong one, you may miss your plane). This is a genuine option situation; you *must* choose even if there is no *rational* way to support your choice or evidence to guide your choice of which route to take to get to the airport on time.

James believed that one could will to have faith in a genuine option situation. Either one chooses to have faith in a particular god or not, so the choice is forced. The choice is living—believing in this god is attractive, so is believing in another god, so is believing in no god at all. Since "you bet your life," the choice is momentous. If this choice is not decidable on purely rational grounds, then this is indeed a genuine option situation. So you make your choice and take your chances.

James thought that a choice made in a genuine option situation made "the will to believe" a legitimate option in matters of faith. But James's view actually legitimates making choices on the basis of *hope.* When we have no way to determine reasonably what is the best *action* to take, whether catching a plane or having faith, if we are in a genuine option situation, then we not only can, but actually must, act on the basis of what we hope is the best choice.

Faith or Hope?

Hope is not faith. Like faith, hope is not compatible with certitude—we cannot hope for what we know will happen. If I throw a ball up in the air a few feet above my head, I cannot *hope* that it will fall back down because I am certain that it will (unless, of course, someone snatches it from the balcony above me or otherwise interferes). Hope is incompatible with certitude.

Hope is always about the future, while faith is not only future oriented. I may hope that my choices and acts have good results, but it seems odd for me to say I have faith that my acts will turn out to be right. I may be certain about the results of my acts and know that they are good, or I may be uncertain and hope they turn out well. But in neither case does it make sense to say I have "faith" in my acts or their outcomes. Although hope is often intimately connected with faith, and particular faiths may even entail particular hopes, hope is not faith.

In sum, the various forms of the moralist misunderstanding of faith as the equivalent of a moral choice or of an act of will are rooted in nineteenth-century conceptions of faith. That our moral dispositions, choices, and habits are related to our faith is clear. But they are not *identical* to our faith, nor the cause of our faith, nor is our faith the only factor in our moral choices. Hence, faith is neither morality nor the same as hope, especially the hope that our moral choices will turn out well.

FAITH AND FEELING

If you have ever participated in a powerful revival service, or been swept up in the frenzy generated by a gifted Pentecostal preacher, or participated in the ecstasy generated by whirling dervishes, you may well understand why people identify faith with religious emotion. Nineteenth-century German Protestant theologian F. D. E. Schleiermacher defined the piety that underlies life in a religious faith tradition as "the feeling of absolute dependence." Many theologians have assumed—not without good reason—that Schleiermacher's "piety" is simply another word for faith. Even if they are correct in their analysis, equating faith with feeling is the *emotionalist* misunderstanding of faith.

Feeling or emotion is certainly a component of faith. Faith without feeling is described as "dry" or "flat" or "dead." But emotion cannot be the whole of faith. Even the most emotional participants in religious traditions recognize that emotions are not sufficient. Emotions may be fleeting; faith is enduring. In the absence of emotion, religious people have spoken of a "dry period" in their faith lives. In the sixteenth century, Saint John of the Cross wrote of a "dark night of the soul" when he had great trouble praying—and when he did, it was profoundly unfulfilling. Moreover, as we discuss the expressions of faith in Chapters 3 and 4, we will see that some expressions of faith have little emotional or affective component—at least on the surface. All these factors indicate that the feeling or emotion is not the substance of faith, even if feeling is a component of faith. Faith is always "faith in . . ."

Emotions and Faith as Relationships

As with the two previous misunderstandings of faith, there are important things to be learned from the emotionalist misunderstanding. First, emotions are relational. We feel *about* something. And this point about faith is crucial. It is a *relationship*. Second, emotions may not be chosen rationally, though not all emotional responses are *irrational*. Whatever the roots of our particular emotions may be, some emotional responses "make sense" while others are puzzlingly "flat" or embarrassingly "overboard."

While we rarely think of emotions as "rational," we do find them "appropriate." We appropriately feel sorrow at the misfortunes of others, joy when our favorite teams win a match or game, grief when a loved one dies. We also talk of some emotions as irrational or inappropriate. For instance, we might say someone has an irrational fear of spiders or an irrational fear of intimacy. We speak of anger as appropriate when it is an emotional response to an intentional injury of a friend, yet we would find it irrational or inappropriate for an adult to be angry with a small child who cannot keep up with the adult's walking pace. Pity or mercy may be warranted or unwarranted. We may find some love irrational or obsessive or silly or beautiful. We respond to emotions—our own or others'—not necessarily "judgmentally" but evaluatively.

Another factor that previous scholars have tended to underplay in discussing faith is that faith is a relationship. But just as emotions relate one to something else, so does faith. Note that Schleiermacher's definition just cited fails to mention *on whom or what* the pious person depends. Saint Thomas Aquinas, the great thirteenth-century theologian whose work is central to Roman Catholic philosophy and theology, argued that faith is a virtue. We ordinarily think of virtues as a person's good habits, not a relationship. Karl Barth, the influential twentieth-century Swiss Protestant theologian whose work is paradigmatic for many Protestant theologians, found that faith is an unearned gift from a gracious God. For Barth, faith is a relationship, but all the work is done by God, none by the recipient. It is construed as a "one-way" relationship. Paul Tillich, a twentieth-century liberal Protestant theologian who influenced many Protestant and not a few Catholic theologians, defined faith as one's "ultimate concern." Some take Tillich to imply that we have another "one-way" relationship, as if we choose our ultimate concern (which was not his point).

None of these theologians would deny that faith involves a relationship. For Aquinas, the virtue of faith is a gift of a gracious God that builds on and completes human abilities and virtues. For Barth, the gift of faith neither builds on nor completes human abilities or virtues, but transforms a human person fundamentally. For Tillich, one's ultimate concern relates one to what is ultimately important for one's life (which may or may not be God). But the fact that one always talks "transitively" about faith as faith *in* something—as a relational term—is not prominent in their works or in scholars' discussions of them.

The emotionalist misunderstanding of faith may be as much a reaction to these theories that seem to downplay the faith relationship as it is an outgrowth of powerful and profound religious feeling. In any case, the emotional misunderstanding alerts us to the relational aspect of faith.

Evaluating Emotions

Even though we think emotions are often not within our control, we nonetheless evaluate emotions rationally by evaluating their appropriateness or inappropriateness in the circumstances. My inference is this: If the expression of emotions that we often think of as irrational or arational or beyond our control can often be rationally evaluated, then why would we think that the expression of faith cannot be rationally evaluated? Obviously, faith can be rationally evaluated just as emotions can—that is the task for Chapter 5.

Yet real faith cannot be reduced to emotions any more than it can be reduced to propositional beliefs or acts of will. We might say, "I was angry with him for an hour after he insulted me, but I got over it." Yet, it would be odd to say, "I had faith in her for about an hour yesterday, but I got over it." Emotions may be fleeting; faith endures.

In sum, that faith has an "affective" or "feeling" or "emotional" component seems clear. But that faith is not merely emotion also seems clear. Yet, like the other misunderstandings of faith, the emotionalist misunderstanding includes insights—feelings are a component of faith and feelings are always about or toward something.

FAITH AND RELIGION

A line I recently heard on a television show has stayed with me. A cop was interrogating an antireligious medical doctor. The doctor was also a murder suspect. A former medical colleague of his, a beautiful woman, had once dated him. She was the victim in the case. But she had long before dumped the doctor to marry a fiery fundamentalist preacher. The cop told the suspect, "She preferred his faith over your science."

The TV cop's words point at both a truth embedded in this misunderstanding and the misunderstanding itself. The truth is that many people see an opposition between science and religion. The misunderstanding is that people who reject religion in the name of science have no faith. This view would be logical if having faith and participating in a religious tradition were the same thing. However, this view presumes that faith and religion are the same thing, that people who have no *religious* faith have no faith. In fact, the committed scientist may well have faith in science.

Faith without Religion

People without religious faith also do have faith. People who do not have faith in personal gods or God often have faith in abstract ideals or concepts. These ideals function for them as the objects of their faith. Religious believers typically have faith in *personal* gods, whereas nonreligious folk have faith in something *impersonal* or *beyond* the personal.

Secular humanism is a form of faith—faith in the fundamental goodness of humanity. Scientific materialism is another humanistic form of faith—faith that science is the source of ultimate truth because there is nothing beyond what science can analyze. Another form of materialism, classical Marxism, was a form of faith; it promoted a faith in the progress of humanity toward realizing a classless society. Adolf Hitler's Nazism was rooted in faith in "blood and soil." These are not forms of *religious* faith, but they are all types of faith. One's faith is not always developed and expressed in the context of a *religious* faith tradition.

Committed religious believers sometimes talk as if humanists and other nonreligious people have no faith. The truth in this is that they do not believe in a god who creates and sustains the world. They do not believe (usually) in hidden spirits, whether divine or demonic, that act in the world. But what they do *not* believe in does not mean they have no faith; rather, the question is, *in what do they place their faith*?

Humanists have faith in humanity. They believe in that which is deepest and best in all of us. What inhibits the best in us from coming out are circumstances that warp or shatter us. Even the most heinous criminal could have been good, save for the circumstances of having a brain disease or a disastrous upbringing or an oppressive life situation. At our best we recognize our limits and live in solidarity with all the others on this earth who are, like us, doomed to live a short while and then die.

The varieties of humanism do not all accept the intrinsic goodness or perfectibility of humanity. Some have faith in science to unlock the secrets of nature, of society, and of the human personality. This form of humanism is usually called *scientific materialism* or *scientism*. It has faith not so much in humanity itself but in human intelligence. Some would argue, though, that science is not a matter of faith, that scientific materialists do not have faith in science. Indeed, they would argue that science is opposed to faith. Two considerations will show why this view is wrong.

Final Fact Parity

First is what we can call "final fact parity." On the one hand, scientific materialists claim that the principles that explain the universe are to be found within the universe. Whatever can be explained is explained by processes that take place within the universe that science investigates. There is nothing outside the universe investigated by science that explains the universe. It cannot be explained—the universe is all there is.

For materialists, the reality of the universe is the final fact. Nothing beyond the universe available to science can (or is needed to) explain it. While things within the universe can be explained, the world as a whole cannot; it just is. To ask where it comes from is to seek an explanation of the inexplicable. Seeking such an explanation is confused. The world is the final fact.

On the other hand, theists—people who believe that God created the universe—deny that the universe is the final fact. Rather, the universe can be explained. It is the effect of a creative act of God. They may claim that God may not be visible to science, but that God's creative act explains the universe on a level deeper than science can reach. But when asked where God comes from, the theist responds that God is *causa sui*, self-caused. To ask the question of where God comes from is a confusion—it assumes that God, who is inexplicable in terms beyond God, can be explained. Theists see God as the final fact, inexplicable in other terms.

So which fact is *final*? God or the world? Both theists and scientific materialists recognize that all explanations end in what is inexplicable. Analyzing the details of the debates between theists and scientific materialists is a practically endless task—not undertaken here. But the net result is an intellectual stalemate. The materialist and the theist seem to be on a par with one another; both push explanation to the limit but find the limit located in different "final" facts. This is "final fact parity."

Final fact parity means that the problem deciding the point at which explanations end is not solvable on purely rational grounds. Both theists and the materialists can develop good arguments for the validity and coherence of their views. However, neither has a knock-down argument for accepting one final fact rather than another. Both theists and materialists have to accept final facts on something like faith. Choosing one over the other may involve a Jamesian "genuine option situation." That is, it may be an exercise of faith or hope, undecidable on purely rational grounds.

The Development Factor

Second, there is a "development factor." Sigmund Freud, the founder of psychoanalysis, developed a major part of his case against religious belief in *The Future of an Illusion* (1927). He argued that religious beliefs were illusions—that is, beliefs that one holds not on the basis of evidence or argument, but only because one wishes them to be true. We wish to have a god to protect us, to give us what we want, and to save us from death. Since we wish a god to rescue us from the ills that beset us, we come to believe that there must be such a being. We have no reason to believe, no evidence to support such a belief, but only a wish that it is true.

On Freud's account, religious belief is as irrational as the belief that I can flap my arms and fly because I *want* that belief to be true. His point was that if religious beliefs are illusions, then the rational thing to do is to abandon them. Rational persons believe what evidence and argument show to be true, not what they merely wish to be true.

What is of interest for us here, however, is not his case for considering religious belief to be illusion, but his rebuttal of a counter-argument that he envisioned religious believers would make against his views. He thought that believers would accuse him of substituting his own emotionally unsatisfying and cold illusion—the illusion of science—for the satisfying and warm illusion of religion. The belief in science, they would argue, is just as much based in the scientists' wish that science would solve the problems of humanity as some religious believers' faith that God will solve all human problems is based in the believers' wish.

Freud responded that science, if it is an illusion, is a different sort of illusion. Unlike religion, he said, science is self-correcting. If a believer in science holds false beliefs, the very work of science can and does correct them. In contrast, Freud believed, religious faith is not merely an illusion but an irrational belief, a delusion because religious belief cannot admit of correction. Hence, even if science were an illusion (and he did not think it was but was willing to accept that view for the purpose of argument), it would be a healthy illusion, not a delusion.

Yet Freud was only partially correct. He was surely correct about *some* religious traditions—those that are fossilized, frozen into unchangeable beliefs. These may be delusions. Yet he was wrong about *other* traditions. Most religious traditions recognize that their formulations of their beliefs, even some of their most central convictions, can require modification in the light of further experience and understanding. The Roman Catholic Church, for example, condemned freedom of conscience in the nineteenth century but advocated it as a political right in the final third of the twentieth century. While religious traditions are not scientific and do not make scientific progress, some faith traditions recognize the need for a "development of doctrine" as those traditions respond to a changing world. Such traditions are not frozen into delusion.

Moreover, religious people grow in wisdom. Many scholars write of faith as a *journey*. We begin with a faith we inherit, a naive faith. We generally accept what we are told. We believe. But then that faith is challenged. We realize, often in adolescence, that the comforting stories told us in our youth are simply not very credible. The evils in the world challenge the notion that God is all-good and all-powerful. The failures of religious or political leaders to be worthy of our trust undermine not only their credibility but the credibility of what they taught us. We discover that other people have different faiths and realize that what we were told was "certain" is opposed by people from other traditions who are wise and good. We have a crisis of faith.

Some of us resolve that crisis by affirming the faith we were taught in a nuanced and critical manner. We accept the tradition we were given as a whole, but we may not buy into some of its parts. We come to a mature, sometimes chastened, faith. We may, for example, accept an Orthodox Jewish tradition as a whole but reject or ignore some of its traditional teachings on particular points.

Others of us reject the tradition we were taught and find a new way of faith. We abandon our Baptist past. We embrace nonreligious humanism or scientific naturalism as our mature faith. We come to have a "new, mature" faith, appropriate for a "rational" person.

These two journeys have different shapes. But they are both journeys of faith, one to a reinvigorated appreciation of "the old faith" and the other to a commitment to a "new creed." Many find new ways to live out their old creeds. But some do move out of the religious tradition they inherited. Indeed, Freud himself began his life in a Jewish family and wound up with faith in science. He may have thought it a rational faith, in contrast to the irrational faith found in religion.

The development factor reminds us that for most of us faith is a quest or a journey. We may remain in or return to our old faith in the end or come to a new faith. We cannot always predict the journey we will take. Freud's argument implicitly shows that those who refuse to journey in faith may be in a faith that is illusory, but not all refuse such a journey. He also implicitly concedes that belief in science can be a form of faith.

Faith and Science

Science may seem opposed to some forms of faith. But it is an opposition of one form of faith to another, of *scientism* or *scientific materialism* to *fundamentalism* or to a faith that God works through and in the world that science explains at one level, but not at the deepest level. Science versus religion is not an opposition of reason to faith. Both humanists and religious believers can exercise reasonableness, but both also exercise faith—in different ways—illustrated by their acceptance of different "final facts" that are inexplicable.

In sum, religion and faith are not identical. Like the fictional detective mentioned above, we tend to take them as identical, perhaps because most people do indeed learn their faith in the context of a particular religious tradition. Yet Nazis' faith in blood and soil or scientists' faith in science or humanists' faith in humanity are clearly faiths that are not learned in the context of religious traditions. Some of us learn what our faith actually is in other contexts. → can come from many different factors

CONCLUSION

The concept of faith is one that is often misunderstood. The pattern of misunderstanding is clear: to take a component of faith as if it were the whole of faith. One cannot separate faith from reason, morality, or emotion. But neither can one reduce faith to reason, morality, or emotion. Nor can one find that faith is simply a matter of religious belief and practice. Faith is not necessarily the enemy of reason or science. Rather, even scientific rationalism seems rooted in faith.

Clearing away the brush of misunderstanding as we have done in this chapter does not display what faith is or how to understand what faith is. That is the subject of Chapter 2.

2

Defining Faith

If faith has been misunderstood in so many ways, how can we understand it more adequately? Some scholars see the *subject* of faith—the one who has faith—as the key. Others have taken the *object* of faith—what one has faith in—as the key. I argue that faith is fundamentally a *relationship* between the one who has faith and that which one has faith in. This approach preserves the insights we developed in the last chapter while eliminating the misunderstandings we uncovered.

Our working definition is that faith is *the relationship between one and the irreducible energizing source of meaning and center of value in one's life*. We shall consider the subject of faith ("one"), the object of faith, and only then the relationship between them. Throughout this chapter we will use love as an analogy to help explore faith. While understanding faith by analogy with love may seem like explaining the difficult (faith) by the unfathomable (love), the analogy is nonetheless apt.

There are, of course, other ordinary uses of *faith* in English and other languages. Generally, usages treat *faith* as equivalent to *trust* or *belief*. There is no doubt that both trust and belief are components of faith. But the use of *faith* as a synonym for *trust* or *belief*, as when someone says, "Have faith in my abilities," is a usage different from the one we are examining here.

PEOPLE OF FAITH

In the last chapter and in the working definition above, I have intentionally used the generic term *one* for the subject of faith.

26

One can designate either an individual person or a group (or sometimes both) as the subject of faith. I have used *one* rather than another term because both individual persons and communities of persons—faith communities—can be the subject of faith. We sometimes talk of "the Catholic faith" if we want to designate the shared faith of those whose faith is shaped by a particular historic religious tradition. At other times, if we want to talk about the faith of particular individuals, we talk of "my faith" or "Jean's faith." By using the term *one*, I want to make sure that we neglect neither individual persons nor communities as the subjects of faith.

Many discussions of the subject of faith focus on an individual person's faith. This approach encourages each of us to reflect on our own faith, to figure out what we have faith in, and to explore the place of our faith in our own lives. This is very good. However, starting with the individual person risks missing the important communal aspect of faith. So we begin with the communal aspect of faith.

The Communal Aspect of Faith

The communal aspect of faith is important. Others teach us *how* to have faith and *how* to understand our faith. We learn how to be faithful from and in communities of faith, even if we may later come to reject the faith those communities have taught us. The insight of (mistakenly) equating faith with religion is that others teach us how to live out a faith. Typically, such teaching occurs in those faith communities that we identify as "religions."

If it seems odd to say we learn "how to have faith," consider that we learn "how to love" another person. As children, our parents give us love in a host of ways. They teach us how to act lovingly toward siblings and others. They guide us as adolescents and young adults learning more mature ways of loving. If we're lucky, that is. All too many are not so lucky. Some children are abandoned by a parent. Abused children may associate violence and beatings with love so strongly that they cannot imagine that someone who does not beat them loves them. Some abused children become abusers of their own children. Some who live in frigid homes never learn how to express affection. Some feel betrayal if their parents divorce and remarry, a feeling that may stunt their ability to love. Some of us—from whatever causes—simply have not learned how to love well. Learning how to love is an accomplishment, but one grounded in what we learn from our parents, family, friends, and society.

Learning how to have faith is also grounded in a community that guides its members to become mature in a faith. Some religious groups, however, discourage reflection on faith and call for obedience, even blind obedience, to the precepts of faith and to the leaders who teach the faith. Like those who have never learned very well what mature love is, those who only "pray and obey" are taught to have an immature, blind faith.

The reaction to such doctrinaire faith can be blind rebellion. People can become convinced that all faith is nonsense or childish or misleading or manipulative. Hence, they reject the very idea of faith. They come to think they have no faith since they rebel against nonsense, eschew childish comforts, and avoid deceptive or manipulative people who demand their obedience. As there may be no way to predict which abused children will learn how to love well and which cherished children will become abusers, so there is no way to predict who will mature in a faith tradition or who will abandon a faith tradition as immature.

Learning how to live maturely in a faith tradition is an accomplishment. Conversion illustrates this point. Conversion is not merely an event but also a process. Converts to a faith tradition have to learn how to practice it and understand it fully. Adapting a phrase from lecture nine of *The Varieties of Religious Experience* (1902) by William James, we can call conversion *a change in the habitual center of one's energy*.

James highlights that a conversion is not so much a loss or gain of faith, but a change in a relationship. What had been the energizing source of meaning and value in one's life is so no longer. When one converts, one must learn *how* to swim in a new stream of faith. One's beliefs and behavior change. One may realize, for example, that one can no longer accept the Bible as the inerrant word of God and drift into secular humanism. One changes as one learns how to live as a secular humanist—something one learns from other secular humanists. As in love, so in faith: a community of "like-minded people" teaches us how to live in and live out a faith.

Rejecting or rebelling against a tradition takes various forms. Typically, challenges to a religious tradition that one has inherited may provoke a crisis of faith or a drifting away from a community of faith. In responding to those challenges, Baptists may backslide, Catholics may lapse, Orthodox Jews may become nonobservant. Or they may reaffirm the faith they were taught. Yet even the ways that people move away from the traditions of their childhood and into other forms of faith show that, like the old faith, the new faith has to be learned from a new community. Whatever faith one moves into involves faith in a new "irreducible energizing center."

Personal Faith

Yet faith is not only a communal enterprise. An individual person may have a distinctive faith and may not associate with a particular faith community. As noted above, scholars often focus on the individual person when discussing the subject of faith.

Remarkable characters reveal much about the journey of faith. Consider Stephen Dedalus, the character James Joyce creates as the protagonist in *A Portrait of the Artist as a Young Man*. Stephen begins his life dominated by a strict Catholic father. He rebels against his faith, sinning prodigiously. After a grueling chapter of hellfire and brimstone sermons, he attempts to live out a stern Irish Catholicism. He is invited to consider becoming a priest. But he comes to his mature faith: he is an artist. He has converted to a faith in beauty and to working to create beauty that will not perish.

Stephen's journey is a variation on a common theme. He begins swimming in a sea of naive faith. As he grows, he enters a turbulent time of rebellion and struggle. He then tries to return to the faith of his naive beginnings—many people do attain a mature faith, one tested by temptation and yet affirmed as one's own. But that was not for Stephen. His path took him to a new faith commitment enriched by his journey and strengthened by his struggle with and against the currents of faith shaping his life.

Each of us has an irreducible source or sources of meaning and value in our life. Something makes my life worth living, even if I cannot quite figure out what it is or express my faith in it very clearly. Sometimes our lives are drab and dull—those centers are hardly energizing at all. Some of us have never had to think about our faith because we have never questioned the faith we were given. And some of us have never thought much about what makes our life worth living, whether we just enjoy life fully or just get by from day to day, swimming happily along as unaware of faith as fish are of water.

Faith and Doubt

Like love, faith ebbs and flows. People of faith encounter difficulties. They are sometimes discouraged. They may even have serious doubts about their faith. Some leave their inherited tradition altogether. Yet some believe that even if faith is a risk, faith is incompatible with doubt. If you have faith, you have no doubts. The great Catholic theologian of the nineteenth century, John Henry Newman, and the influential Protestant theologian of the twentieth century, Paul Tillich, explored how faith and doubt are related.

In his *Apologia pro Vita Sua*, John Henry Newman gave an account of his own journey of faith away from Anglicanism to Roman Catholicism. He wrote that "ten thousand difficulties do not make one doubt." Newman believed faith to be a gift of God. Hence, he found that to doubt one's faith meant to doubt God. Of course, Newman could recognize the difficulties that a person of faith has. But all the difficulties (subjectively) one has does not mean that one loses one's faith by doubting God. Newman's sort of reasoning has led some religious leaders, even today, to say that doubt is a sin.

Paul Tillich, writing a century later, argued that there is no faith without doubt. Tillich meant *doubt* not as doubt of the object of faith but as designating the uncertainties, worries, difficulties, trials, and confusions a person of faith has. Tillich argued that faith required courage. A person of faith has to have courage to have faith in the face of uncertainty, to overcome the trials, and to work through the confusions to achieve clarity. Even when one does so, one can never be entirely certain in faith, that is, that one has rightly placed one's faith in the right object of faith. As noted in Chapter 1, faith is a risk—an unavoidable one. For Tillich, the opposite of faith is despair. While we have claimed that no person lives without faith, Tillich rightly highlights that those who fail to have the courage to affirm their faith finally may fall into despair. Despair is not merely the experience of a "dark night" or emptiness. To live without courage is to live without effective faith and without real hope for the future. Despair is the end stage of faithlessness; it is spiritual death. When one is in despair, one may try to escape by turning to drugs or mindless activity. But sometimes the ultimate escape of suicide seems the only way out. For when one has no energizing center of meaning or source of value in one's life, how can one live?

This linguistic difference between Newman and Tillich over doubt is not due merely to their writing in different centuries. Newman thought faith to be a gift; the only object of faith was God, because only God could give one true faith. Newman wrote with a very particular Roman Catholic concern about doubt in mind. To doubt faith, in his view, was to doubt God, who gave the faith. Thus, to doubt faith was to lose faith in God. In contrast, Tillich took faith to be one's ultimate concern; the religious and secular faith traditions of the world proposed many objects of faith. He wrote about faith in the context of the variety of faith traditions. For him, faith was not so much a gift of God but a person's fundamental state of mind and heart.

Newman's and Tillich's different understandings of faith highlight the different emphases in their work. Newman focused on the reasonableness of belief in the object of faith. Tillich highlighted the existential and psychological situation of the subject of faith. However, Newman's difficulties and Tillich's doubt are not so different from each other: Both concern the subject of faith.

Tillich, however, highlights the need for courage in faith; Newman displayed courage but wrote little about it. To take a risk requires courage. Especially in the face of the uncertainty of faith, given the many options open to one, courage is clearly a component of faith. But this uncertainty is due to the many possible objects of faith that one faces.

Both Newman and Tillich thought that there was only one true god. Newman believed the true god was God, that is, the creator, redeemer, and sustainer of the world revealed in and through the Christian tradition. For Tillich, the true god was God, that is, the truly Ultimate experienced in many ways and expressed in many images, especially including those images of God found in his own Christian tradition. Both had faith in the same god, but under different descriptions. Each lived out that faith in different ways. And each would reject lesser gods because they were inadequate objects for authentic faith.

Yet neither Newman nor Tillich could have full certainty about his stream of faith. Even they recognized that they might be mistaken, though they did not believe they were actually in error. At this point we can recognize their views about true faith but cannot (yet) accept them. At this point we must keep our minds open and examine the various gods that people have faith in. And from this point on, we shall take *doubt* and *difficulties* as basically synonymous terms to describe one's struggles with the challenges to one's faith.

THE GOD(S) OF FAITH

The appropriate designator for the object of the faith relationship is *a god*. To paraphrase contemporary theologian Nicholas Lash, as our treasure is whatever we value, so a god or gods is whatever we have faith in. I would add that just as one person's trash is another's treasure, so one person's idol may be another's god. What one person takes as an illusion can be another's true god. Here's a definition: One's god or gods are the irreducible source(s) of meaning and center(s) of value in one's life.

We do not always recognize our actual god or gods. However, we can come to recognize our god or gods when we consider the questions about what gives meaning and value to our lives. When we can find no more answers that have any more content than "just because," we may recognize (or are close to recognizing) what is the source of meaning and value, our god.

How We Learn of Our Gods

If every one of us has a god or gods, how do we come to have them? Gods are like ideas, values, and ideals. We get all of these from our social context. Our culture teaches us, for example, that slim bodies are beautiful. The more voluptuous bodies painted by Peter Paul Rubens (1577–1640) may have been idealized in his time, but the Rubenesque body is out of style now. In our culture, no one wants to be fat. We are bombarded with advertisements for diet products. Some of us internalize this ideal in helpful ways—we watch our diet and exercise. Some of us internalize this ideal in harmful ways—we are bulimic or anorexic. But the culturally produced image of the ideal body really becomes *my* ideal. In our culture, we each want to have a slim or slimmer body. Today, none of us would say, as one with a Rubenesque ideal might say, "I am not plump enough yet to have a great body." *The ideal* is a social construct; *my* ideal results from the ways in which I internalize (or resist) that socially given ideal.

The *images* we have of the gods are social constructs (this does not mean that the gods are necessarily social constructs; that's a different issue). They are "external" to us. Yet we make them *our* god or gods as we internalize them as the irreducible sources of meaning and centers of value that energize each of *our* lives. Few, if any, of us have faith in Thor or Hera or Jove. They are "out of style" in our culture. The gods that appeal to us may be "our Father in heaven," our nation, humanity, and so on. These images are social constructs; how we come to have faith in a god or gods is through a process of personal integration—a process we may not even be aware of. *My* god is surely mine, but it is also one that my culture has made available for me to imagine as a possible object of faith (and the broader my cultural understanding, the broader the range of possibilities may well be).

If my god or gods are unique, I might even be able to speak of *my* theology. Of course, most of us have a god or gods that we share with others. We are Lutherans or Muslims or Zen Buddhists or secular humanists or. . . . Most of us participate, however loosely, in a tradition that has shown us a god or gods worth having faith in. However nontraditional I may be, however distinctive the god or gods I have faith in are, however idiosyncratic my personal understanding of the center of meaning and value in my life may be, my theology cannot be purely subjective—else I could not speak of those gods at all. Even *my* theology must use a language that *I* have learned and that *we* share if I am to be able to speak of the god or gods I have faith in.

Our Gods, Our Values, Our Worship

A god is not necessarily a thing. That is, a god is not necessarily an object in the empirical world in the sense that my spouse is the object of my love or a new motorcycle is the object of my desire. To designate a god as the object of faith is simply to designate whatever it might be that one has faith in. To say faith *has* an object is to say that faith is *transitive*. Just as emotions have an object, so faith has an object.

The gods people have faith in are not necessarily personal. As we noted in Chapter 1, the gods may be lofty ideals, like justice or truth. They may be those things that our culture teaches us are the most important things to have, like money or success or power. Many in our culture have faith in these gods. The gods may be creators of the world or powers in the world, spoken of in imaginative or literal ways, worshiped explicitly or implicitly. The variety of the gods and the ways we think of them, speak of them, and act toward them— that is, how we worship them—is astounding.

What makes them *our* gods is the relationship *we* have with them. Whatever is (are) the irreducible, energizing center(s) of value and source(s) of meaning in our lives is (are) our gods. Our gods are not just our ideals—they are what make our ideals ideal. Our gods are not just our goals—they are what make our goals worth pursuing.

What makes something our *god* is that it is the *source* of what is meaningful and valuable in our lives. Some people value justice as an ultimate or irreducible ideal; justice may well be their god. Some value justice because God does. For them, God is the source that makes justice their value. The differences between the two groups may be very small in practice. Both will work for justice. But what makes them different is that they have different irreducible energizing centers that are the sources of their strength even as they work together. Even though they have different *sources* of meaning and value, different gods, they may work for similar values.

A god is what we worship. *Worship* is a strange verb. We usually equate it with what we do in church or temple or private prayer. We often equate it with religious ritual. But this is too limited an understanding of *worship*. To worship is to engage in those practices that express our relationship to our god or gods. Misers worship money; their form of worship is hoarding it. Some patriots worship their country; they will go to war to kill their enemies, lustily sing the national anthem, and salute the flag unreservedly. Secular humanists worship humanity; their worship is to work for the flourishing of all humankind. The *ways* people worship are as varied as the gods worshiped. If something is one's god, one is not passive but works on the relationship in appropriate ways, as a lover works on his or her relationship with the beloved.

Sacrifice is also an aspect of worship. Sacrifice is letting go of something valuable to seek something more valuable. The miser may sacrifice love to have his gold, the patriot may sacrifice her life willingly for the good of the country, and the secular humanist may deny himself the comfort of religious communities and belief in God. Sacrifices are not always hard. But whatever god I have faith in places some goods out of my reach. Those who make athletic achievement at a very high level the center of meaning and source of value in all they do will have to sacrifice some creature comforts. As worship is the activity of faith, so sacrifice is the abstinence of faith—to worship one god means one must give up having some goods not so valuable to the god that is the source of meaning and value in one's life.

One's faith shapes one's life. We sometimes think of active faith in terms of spirituality. A spirituality is the set of practices that constitutes our relationships to our gods, our faith in practice. Our spirituality is both how we worship and what we must sacrifice to be faithful to our gods. The ancient tale of King Midas displays the spirituality of a miser.

To call the object of faith "irreducible" means that it is the *ultimate* source of meaning and value. Most of us, of course, have many values. We value our family and our country and our friends and our lovers. But we can ask these questions: What would be of value if these were gone? What would have meaning if these were meaningless? If the accurate answer is "nothing," then we have reached our *irreducible source* or *sources* of value and center or centers of meaning. We have found our true gods! The key issue in discovering the object of one's faith is its irreducibility.

Most religious traditions are explicit in saying that God or the gods are the Source or sources of meaning and value. Those of us who participate in one of the Christian traditions, for example, should accept that all that is valuable to us is valuable because it is rooted in being valued by God. Those of us who participate in Theravadan Buddhist traditions should see everything as valuable and every truth as meaningful, but that each in its proper place is *ultimately* valuable in and of itself, not because its value and meaning are derived from or dependent on any other particular source. Of course, good Buddhists and good Baptists find real joy and happiness in their relationships with friends and families. The point is not to deny the meaningfulness or the value of such relationships but to ask what is the *irreducible source* of meaning and value that grounds the meaning of these relationships.

We may never have thought about our faith or we may think that we have none. Some of us say that our god is the god of our religious faith tradition—and we may be wrong about that! How many nominal Christians are really misers who actually worship the god called "wealth"? For many of us, discovering our real god or gods requires serious searching. Where can we begin? This is the existential question: What do we really believe in when all is said and done?

Discovering Our Gods

The first question we can ask to help discern the object of our faith, our god or gods, is: For what do we live? What energizes our life? The second question is, perhaps, even more telling: What would we die for? Why would we die for that?

Characters portrayed in novels, dramas, and biographies often display what they live for. Some authors make the point of their work to show how a character—typically the hero or villain—comes to realize what he or she lives for. Others show the faith of a character more or less in passing.

In *Sense and Sensibility*, for example, Jane Austen shows Elinor and Marianne Dashwood coming to realize not only what love is, but just whom they love. But Austen also portrays a deceptive (and possibly self-deceptive) character in the very attractive, but dissolute and fickle, John Willoughby. Before the time of the novel Willoughby has fathered an illegitimate child and abandoned the child and her mother. During the novel his affectionate words and deeds encourage Marianne to believe that he is in love with her, but he coldly abandons her to marry Miss Grey, a rich young woman whom he does not love. Miss Grey's position and wealth are Willoughby's reward, because they make possible what he lives for—a life of luxury and convenience. When Marianne is ill later in the novel, Willoughby rushes to her sick room, showing that he realizes what might have been. But the very moderate financial resources that Marianne could bring to marriage could not pay for the luxuries he lived for. Given the choice of wealth without love or love without wealth, he revealed his true faith. He sacrificed any love he had for Marianne. He may rue the day he spurned Marianne, but he could not have both her love and his pleasures. To get what he worshiped, he had to sacrifice any attachment to her.

Willoughby is the villain in the novel and the films and television serials based on it. He shows the ruthlessness of a cad who selfishly devotes his life to pleasure. For Willoughby, we can say that pleasure is his god, an *irreducible* center that gives meaning and value to all he knows, does, and is. Everyone and all things that do not contribute to his pleasure are not important to him. If his relationships with them significantly obstruct his quest for pleasure, he must sacrifice them. They are of little value in his sight because he places his faith in a god whom they do not serve.

Austen portrays Willoughby in contrast to Marianne and Elinor Dashwood. Each of them overcomes her illusions and comes to have both sense and sensibility. The novel ends with them living happily, if not lavishly, ever after. After trials and tribulation, they find themselves in love with good men who become their respective husbands.

Communities as well as individuals have gods. The Nazis of Austria and Germany in the 1930s and 1940s lived in and lived out a tradition that made "blood and soil"—unbounded devotion to nationality and land—an energizing center of meaning and value. This ethnic faith with its genocidal corollary rejected the humanity of others not seen as children of the valued blood and soil. The Nazis were neither the first nor the last to have such a faith. Nor were they the first or last to commit genocide. Nazism exemplifies patriotism deified. When one's country becomes one's god, it can do no wrong; wherever the government leads is the right place to go, even if it leads its citizens to murder.

The differences in the gods we worship are significant. Scholars have classified them in order to analyze the characteristics of different forms of faith.

Classifying Faiths: For What Does One Live?

We can place the varieties of faith into three major categories: polytheistic, henotheistic, and universalist. A number of different streams of faith can be identified in each category.

It is often difficult to distinguish among these types in practice. However, we can use as a handy guide the "Golden Rule test": "Do unto others as you would have them do unto you." All religious traditions of which I am aware prescribe some version of this rule. The great philosopher Immanuel Kant (1724–1804) made a philosophical version of the rule the center of his moral theory. Here I will not argue for or against the significance of the rule. I simply intend to use the Golden Rule as a test to distinguish types of faith by showing how participants in each of the types understand who are the "others" to be done unto. So the "Golden Rule test" is not about morality but about vision: Whom do we see as "others" worthy of moral treatment under a

Golden Rule? Whom do we see as beyond the range of the rule? That is the test.

It is also important to distinguish the kinds of faith. This analytical tool helps us see if there are differences between the ways a faith is described in theory and how it is lived in practice. Judaism, Christianity, and Islam, for example, are officially monotheistic. Yet, as we shall see, some Christians are polytheists. Some Jews, ethnic Christians, and Muslims live out a henotheistic faith. Such disparities lead us to ask if the real, lived faith of a person or community is faithful to the tradition that teaches one the faith.

Polytheism

Some of us are energized by multiple gods. One may live for nation and power and pleasure, devoting oneself to one or the other depending on different circumstances. We go with the flow of the current of the moment. We seek love in the family, wealth in business, and power in the community. Nothing welds them together. They are just the irreducibly different parts of our lives. Each has an irreducibly different source of value and center of meaning. We may be clever and balanced enough to avoid letting concerns from one sphere bleed over into another area. Those of us who have faith in multiple irreducible centers of value and meaning can be called *polytheists* (*poly* is "many" in Greek; *theos* is the Greek word "god").

Ancient Romans offered sacrifices to the goddess Ceres for the success of the crops, invoked the god Mars for winning military victories, and worshiped the emperor as the divine representation of the state. This form of polytheism may not have taken the gods to be the *sources* of meaning and value but rather the *powers* that could ensure that what was held meaningful and valuable would thrive. Yet these ancient gods symbolize some of the sources of meaning and value—food (to eat and sell), land (to dominate or exploit), safety, and a state that keeps all in order. Today, people may not worship particular deities. Yet people do show what their gods are by how they live their lives.

For example, novelist Mario Puzo portrayed in *The Godfather* a Mafia leader who had grown from an impoverished teen-aged fugitive from Italy into a powerful American citizen devoted to both family and power. He had some serious moral standards: he was sexually faithful to his wife, refused to deal in drugs, and attempted to reason with his opponents before resorting to lethal action in order to deal with their refusals to be reasonable. Nominally a Roman Catholic, the godfather, Don Vito Corleone, pays little attention to *pezzonovanti*, the "big shots" of the government or the church. Rather, he is a polytheist. He is devoted to different gods, different centers of meaning and value, in different spheres of his life. He would claim to be a Catholic, but even if God was one of his gods, he surely had faith in money and power as well. He was a polytheist. He believed in gods other than God.

Polytheists have faith in many gods—gods for the many spheres of their lives. Which god they have faith in at any time or place depends more on the circumstances of their lives than on the gods that are the irreducible energizing centers of their lives. Political leaders may be effective and upright in office but incorrigibly sexually promiscuous; they serve both the gods of the polis and of lust. Religious leaders may be wise and insightful in their public roles but hardhearted martinets in the internal affairs of their organizations. For them, serving their "official" god is all too easily compatible with serving the god of personal power and authority.

The Golden Rule test doesn't apply very well to polytheists. In general, polytheists are tolerant to the point of indifference. But whereas for the other types of faith (as we shall see), the rule encourages action for others ("*Do* unto others . . ."), the polytheists' rule is typically more limited, something like "Don't get in my way, and I won't get in yours." In fact, it is hard to imagine polytheists with serious moral *principles*, rather than pragmatic *tactics* that mimic morality, tactics applicable just when necessary. Polytheists tend to avoid applying morality to anyone and having anyone apply it to them. Following the Golden Rule may be good tactics for polytheists, but it is not a moral rule.

Some would say that the issue is tolerance. Polytheists seem to embody tolerance. Yet tolerance is not the issue. Many people are rather tolerant—some even think that an attitude of tolerance that supports (rather than is indifferent to) others is a virtue. If tolerance is a virtue, people of every type of faith possess it—at least with regard to specific others.

Of course it seems hardly an exercise in spirituality to be devoted to some of the gods that win polytheists' devotion. Yet even if a _traditional_ spirituality is missing from polytheism, polytheists nonetheless exercise a certain spirituality, a diligence in the practice of a faith. The asceticism of the celibate monk is not the asceticism of the greedy investor or the wine lover. Don Corleone's devotion to business and family is quite different from his wife's devotion—she attends mass daily to pray for his soul and save him from hell. Yet even polytheists have a sort of spirituality and at least have to sacrifice the single-minded faith in any one god.

Despite being a Catholic of sorts, Vito Corleone worshiped other gods. Discovering the real shape of my faith is not always easy or comfortable. Yet if I realize what I actually live for, I can begin to see the real shape of my life, to understand the gods that give my life meaning and value. And if I have faith in many irreducible sources of value, I am a polytheist.

Henotheism

Those who have faith in _one_ irreducible, but limited, energizing center of value and meaning—"blood and soil" or other national gods, for example—while recognizing that other people have other gods can be called _henotheists_ (_heno_ is one of the Greek words for "one"). There are two types of henotheists.

Tribalists are henotheists who have faith in the god of a particular group, typically a national or ethnic group. German Nazis believed in German blood and soil and believed that others— French, Belgians, Canadians, Russians—gave the same status to their own blood and soil. They sought to conquer Europe and to make Europe "Judenrein" (Jew free) as part of their faith in practice. Tribalism is faith in one god, while recognizing that other groups or tribes have faith in other gods. Whether those others are enemies to be conquered or friends and allies is irrelevant.

Particularists are those who have faith in one ideal while recognizing that others have other ideals. Politicians, for example, may live for power, people in business for success, crusaders for justice, hedonists for pleasure, detectives and scientists for truth, and so forth. Particularists may cooperate with people of other faiths; for example, business folk and politicos often form tactical alliances. To have faith in one particular god may not mean rejecting those who have faith in other gods, at least when cooperation is convenient. It does mean that the worth of everything is measured by how it serves one's particular god.

In each of these patterns of faith we can see the answer to the question, What does one live for? Particular and tribal henotheists have faith in a single, particular god that gives meaning and value to their lives. They recognize that others have other gods, but they have faith only in their own god (as pleasure-seeking Willoughby recognized love as a possible god but continued to place his wager on pleasure).

If henotheists were commanded to observe the Golden Rule, they would do so only pragmatically. The "others" typically would be limited to those who share their faith. A henotheistic patriot may care little about others outside the circle of fellow patriots. A henotheistic businesswoman may lie to those outside her particular company or industry but not to her inner circle. In war, a tribalist may torture the enemy, but not those on his side. Henotheists can and do make alliances of convenience with those of other faiths. They might well treat their allies as part of the "others" of the Golden Rule. For henotheists, the "others" of the Golden Rule exclude those of other faiths. The only constraint on henotheists is not a moral one, but the fear that the outsiders might turn the tables on them.

Hence, a tribalist patriot may not torture enemies so as to avoid giving enemies an excuse to torture his compatriots. The particularist devoted to success in business may lie to competitors but not to politicians who will contribute to her company's success. If henotheists refrain from lying to and torturing outsiders, they refrain not because it is morally wrong to do such things to others, but only because the others might pay them back in their own coin.

Consider the Geneva Conventions, which limit the range of violent practices combatants can undertake in war. Henotheists will want to be seen to follow them, but would just as soon violate them because enemies are not valued. For henotheists, when applied to insiders "Do unto others" is a moral principle, but it is a purely self-serving handy guide to avoiding worse being done to ones' own by others outside one's circle when applied to outsiders.

↳ more of group

Universalisms

In contrast to the varieties of henotheism are the various forms of *universalism*. Universalists have faith in one, universal, irreducible energizing center of value and meaning *and* recognize no other irreducible centers. This is the common thread among the forms of universalism. While the gods of henotheism are limited, the gods of universalism are unlimited sources of meaning and centers of value. The categories of universalism include various religious monisms and monotheisms, religious naturalisms, secular humanism, and various forms of materialism.

Monotheism. Judaism, Christianity, and Islam are supposed to be monotheistic traditions. Most monotheists believe that God created and sustains the world. God is the irreducible source of meaning and center of value for all that there is. God is not simply an object in the world or an aspect of the world. Rather, God is in some sense personal and yet beyond the natural and social world we inhabit. How God is personal, beyond the world, and yet active on and in the world is the subject of lively debate among those monotheists—and has been debated for millennia!

Nonetheless, many Jews, Christians, and Muslims are really henotheists or polytheists. What distinguishes monotheistic faith from henotheistic faith is the way each accepts the first of the Ten Commandments found in the Bible, "I am the Lord, thy God; thou shalt not have strange gods before me." Monotheists accept the first commandment as requiring either rejecting other gods or regarding them as valuable only insofar as they receive value from God, the true irreducible source and center of meaning and value. In contrast, henotheists take the first commandment as a warning that there are strange gods, but we are not to revere them—they are the gods of "other tribes."

Jews, Christians, and Muslims worship the same God. What makes them different is the way they image God and the kinds of faith relationships they have with God. Neither Jews nor Muslims recognize the Christians' image of the Holy Trinity as an appropriate way to talk of God. Neither Christians nor Jews accept the Islamic Qur'an as the final revelation of God. Neither Christians nor Muslims think that God's revelation is final and complete in the Hebrew Bible (which Christians call the Old Testament). To make this even more complex, participants in each tradition have different kinds of relationship with God. But what joins them is the monotheistic precept; they each accept the first commandment in the same way.

Monism. Monism is a form of universalism that believes that all-that-is finally is One. One form of monism is associated with some Hindu religious traditions. Some of them see everything as or as a manifestation of Brahman. The goal of life is to understand that one's soul *(atman)* is the same as the "soul" of the universe (Brahman). The various gods and goddesses found in the Hindu traditions are seen as forms of Brahman. Hinduism is thus not a polytheism but a polymorphic monism—the One takes many forms.

Monisms are different from monotheism in at least two important ways. First, in monism the Ultimate may not be personal, whereas God is intensely personal in monotheism. Second, how one relates to the Ultimate differs. For monists, the goal is conceived as absorption into or union with the infinite. The goal of living is to be absorbed into the infinite as a drop of water is absorbed into the ocean. For monotheists, the goal is conceived as communion with or living eternally in the presence of God. Monotheists do not wish to lose their personhood in absorption into the Ultimate, but to be or become people who can continue their enduring relationship with God eternally.

Monism and monotheism develop different patterns of spirituality. Yet both are species of religious universalism. But there are other types of universalism as well.

Naturalism. Another form of universalism is *naturalism.* There are many other uses of the terms *naturalist* and *naturalism,* but those are not of concern here. Whereas monotheists believe in one universal, transcendent, personal God, the faith of naturalism is in a universal value that is typically *not* personal and *not* transcendent of nature, but a universal value in the natural order. Secular humanists are naturalists in that they find humanity an irreducible source of meaning and center of value. Scientific materialists are prime examples of nonreligious naturalism, too, in that they find the whole of the world as a source of meaning and center of value.

Although we rarely think of them as such, some Buddhists, especially those in the Theravadan traditions, are also naturalists. Every sentient being is valuable. Some Westerners have called those Buddhists *atheists* because they have no gods. This is not quite accurate. These Buddhists find Buddha a human being who pointed the way to *nirvana*, the cessation of desire that gets one proximate and ultimate peace. These Buddhists may not believe in personal gods. But if a god is an irreducible center of meaning and source of value, then such Buddhists are better classified as naturalists, for everything is natural (a concept of "the natural" not shared by Western materialists) and valuable just because it is.

For these Buddhists, even the doctrine of karma is natural. It is part of the way things are. Whatever we do has an effect on us. That effect may be felt in this life or in a future life. There is no god necessary for karma to work. It is just a part of the way things are. That this view of nature is different from the modern Western view seems obvious. But karma is not in some way separate from the natural world but is a real law of nature.

Naturalisms may be religious or nonreligious. What they share is a denial of a supernatural being that creates the world and guides it or enforces its laws. They differ in how they image the irreducible source of meaning and value, how human beings are to live, and what are the outcomes of human deeds.

Universalisms and the Golden Rule Test

For universalists, the Golden Rule applies universally. Whether applied to all humans, all sentient beings, or all things bright and beautiful, there are no exceptions. We are to do unto *every* other as we would want every other to do unto us. It applies to friends and enemies alike. We are not merely to let others go their merry way. Rather, we are to do for them and to them as we wish they would do to and for us.

In contrast to a henotheist, a monotheist or naturalist who goes to war does not observe the Geneva Conventions merely out of self-protection. Rather, a universalist recognizes that such respect is due to all human beings, even the enemy in combat. If a limited application of the Golden Rule is a symptom of henotheism, as discussed above, in contrast, the universality of its application is characteristic of the various forms of monotheism, monism, and naturalism.

In sum, the key to understanding the shape of my faith is how I value the status of the "other": Do I apply the Golden Rule morally because all beings are worthy of my care, as do universalists, or merely tactically to make sure that I don't lose my own advantages, as henotheists do? Resolving this question is one way to see the real shape of my faith.

Classifying Faiths: For What Would One Die?

Beyond the question "what does one live for?" is a second question that helps order our values and points a bit more usefully to what we take to be god: For what would one die?

This question is important because life is the only disease with a 100 percent mortality rate. We are all going to die. Many of us will simply die *of* some accident or disease or disability. What I die *of* will not lend meaning or value to my death. But if I could die *for* something, would that not give my death meaning and value? So answering the question, "What would be worth not only giving my life *to*, but giving my life *for*?" helps me discern the energizing center of meaning and source of value in my life.

In the years before he became the second secretary-general of the United Nations in 1953, the Swedish statesman Dag Hammarskjöld evidently suffered through a multi-year crisis of faith. Before that crisis resolved itself, he wrote in his journal (probably on New Year's Day in 1953—the journal was posthumously published in English translation as *Markings*), "Give me something to die for! . . . Pray that your loneliness may spur you into finding something to live for, great enough to die for." He did die while leading a U.N. peacekeeping mission attempting to mediate a violent dispute in Africa. In 1961 the plane carrying him and fifteen others was shot down near the border between what is now the Democratic Republic of the Congo and Zimbabwe. He died in a quest to keep the peace among and within nations. As one becomes acquainted with Hammarskjöld's story, one realizes that he was willing to die for the sake of peace among all God's people. *Markings* shows the shape of his monotheistic Christian faith. While he had tremendous difficulties with his faith, he lived for what he was willing to die for.

Many of us live for things we would not consider dying for. We live for what those things can do for us, not what we could do for them.

If I find no one and nothing meaningful—no person, no country, no religious community—unless it gratifies me, then I am condemned to loneliness. Everything else is valuable only as it serves me. There is nothing I would die for. For I am a narcissist.

One version of the Greek myth of Narcissus tells of a prophecy about a beautiful young man: if he ever saw his reflection in a still pond, he would die. The first time he did see himself, he reached out to caress the beauty he saw, lost his balance, fell in the water, and drowned. Narcissus loved no one and nothing but himself. No one and nothing meant anything to him. He was his own and only center of meaning and source of value.

But if I think narcissism is "true for me," can I think it is or should be true for everyone? If I think it is "true for all" or simply "true," then why would I think that others should live for me or even sacrifice themselves for me or even love me? Why should anyone care what matters to me? If I'm a narcissist, I cannot really care for anyone else in any serious way. They aren't of real or intrinsic value but only of value to me as instruments contributing to my good. That is, there can be no community of narcissists; each worships his or her own god and cannot share a center of value or source of meaning.

A narcissist can have no equals. Each alone is the irreducible source of value or meaning. Oh, a narcissist might briefly feel the loss of a lover, as did Willoughby over Marianne, but that loss is easily overcome by the next love or other pleasure. A narcissist simply finds a new tool, a new valuable instrument. Mature and lasting mutual love is impossible for a narcissist.

Narcissists are not polytheists. Polytheists have faith in many gods, the narcissist only in one—myself. What marks narcissism as different from henotheism is that the henotheist's god is not himself or herself but a cause that gives the henotheist's life meaning. Henotheists and polytheists can form communities of faith in the same gods; narcissists cannot.

Moreover, for narcissists, the Golden Rule cannot apply as a moral guide. Why would I care how I treat others, except, perhaps, for pragmatic reasons? In fact, narcissists may well be con artists in their relations with others, duping them into thinking that they care for them when what they care about is what others can do for them. Like a henotheist, a narcissist treats the in-crowd and the out-crowd differently. But for a narcissist, the in-crowd has a population of one.

Few of us are narcissists. We may be the centers of our own worlds, but we also recognize that every other planet also has its own gravitational pull, sometimes strong enough to move us out of our normal orbit. We can imagine sacrificing our lives trying to rescue a drowning child. We can imagine dying heroically on the battlefield defending our nation. We can imagine risking our lives to give a kidney to our sister. We may know stories of men and women executed by political authorities because of their religious loyalties. We may have heard the story of Saint Maximilian Kolbe, a Polish conventual Franciscan priest who traded places with Franciszek Gajowniczek, a Jewish family man arbitrarily being sent to his death in the notorious Auschwitz concentration camp in 1941. Most of us can imagine something we might die for, something worth living for; at least we can imagine others who have given their lives for a cause. We recognize that others' lives have meaning and value far beyond their instrumental value to our own satisfaction. For Kolbe, his devotion to God led him to sacrifice his life for another man, a stranger to him.

Why would we or they *die* for something? What makes a drowning child or invaded nation or dying sister or religious faith or condemned stranger or peace among nations worth risking—and perhaps sacrificing—one's life for? As we answer that question we start on our journey to discover and understand both our own way of faith and the object of our faith, the *irreducible* energizing center. When we have exhausted the questions and can find no more answers that have any more content than "just because," we may have finally understood what our god is.

Most of us do find life worth living because of the good things we enjoy. Even those who are oppressed and outcast can usually find times for celebrating life. Few of us are so blinded to the joys, sufferings, and happiness of others that we find ourselves unable to relate to others in the world. We do tend to subscribe to a form of the Golden Rule. While we do suffer in various ways, most of us find life worth living despite our grief and sufferings. The loss of family, friends, lovers, and valued items is sad. But when we can discover what we cannot live without or what we would die for, then we can finally see the root of the meaning and value in our lives. Then we can come to understand the object of our faith. We can learn to which gods we are really devoted.

THE RELATIONSHIP OF FAITH

If the subject of faith is a person or community and the object of faith is a god, an energizing center of meaning and value, then the subject of faith and the object of faith are finally inseparable. We can distinguish persons from their god or gods in theory. But in reality we cannot talk of one without the other. Even the previous two sections could not talk of one without the other. Each section above focused on one side of the relationship as a way of distinguishing the object and subject of faith, but it could not avoid bringing the other side into the discussion as well. So what is that relationship?

Faith and Love

The relationship of faith is analogous to the relationship of love. Love is a relationship between one and another. We often think of love in romantic terms, of the love between two people who are in love with each other. We also talk of the love between parents and child, the often difficult love between siblings, and a host of other loves. Each of these loves develops over time. My relationship with my spouse is far richer now than it was when we were married forty years ago. Our relationships with our daughters have certainly developed over the years. As with love, faith evolves.

What is common to the various ways of speaking of love is that love is a relationship that endures. To say one was "in love" for ten minutes is silly. Or to say, "I loved chocolate for ten minutes yesterday, but then I loved licorice for a half hour, and then peaches for fifteen minutes" is also silly. We might say that we thought we were in love for a while. That's different; we admit to being deceived or confused or overenthusiastic. A love that does not endure long is a passing fancy, not love.

Like love, faith is also an evolving and enduring relationship. It is not static. A child's faith is not an adult's; those who have recently undergone a conversion have a faith that will be different the more they understand the meaning and value that that faith gives them. Faith is not a passing whim or emotion, a concept grasped momentarily and quickly forgotten, an act performed quickly and thoughtlessly. My faith is not a shallow relationship. Indeed, it may be buried so deeply that it is hard for me to discern whether I am a polytheist, henotheist, or universalist. Until I realize the shape of my worship and sacrifice, my spirituality, my faith, may be blind.

The faith of a polytheist may shift from one god to another as a polytheist's concerns shift. The polytheist is like the promiscuous lover who is always with the one he loves because he always loves the one he's with (whoever it may be). However, the *pattern* of polytheistic faith is nonetheless enduring. As the promiscuous lover has a promiscuous pattern of loving, the polytheist has a pattern of having faith in whatever god he or she needs at any given time or for any given circumstances.

Typically, a polytheist is constantly devoted to the same god in each of the spheres of life. The ancient Roman polytheist sacrificed to Mars for success in war (but not love), to Venus for love (but not war), and to Ceres for agricultural abundance (but not love or war). The polytheist, like all of us, moves among spheres like home and family, work, leisure, and so on. But rather than having a single center of value and source of meaning that gives value to all of them, the polytheist finds many different gods, each governing a sphere of life. The polytheist seems to sacrifice the possibility of having an integrated faith.

The Components of Faith

Even those who misunderstand faith intellectually, emotionally, volitionally, or religiously recognize that faith endures, if not for life, then for substantial parts of our lives. Their misunderstandings, however, give us insight into the kind of relationship faith is. Like love, faith has evolving and enduring intellectual, volitional, and emotional components.

To love another, one must understand the other to some degree. One person may never understand another fully. Surely parents and their children seem never to understand each other completely. But if they understood nothing about who the other was—what made the other tick—then how could they love the other? And so with faith. One understands what success or pleasure is. One can understand what one's country or political party stands for. One can attempt to understand the gods one believes in, however partially and inadequately—no Christians in their right minds claim to understand adequately the Trinitarian God they have faith in, despite some insight into who and what this god is (often reached by the way of negation—saying what God is not). But how could one have faith in what one had *no* understanding of?

To love another, one must wish the other well. The feelings or emotions associated with love are varied. They may range from pure lust to gentle patience to amused tolerance to frustration and annoyance. They may be intense or placid. But it would be baffling for one to say that one loved another but had little or no feelings or emotions about the beloved. And so with faith. Faith may be a quiet blessed assurance, an intense satisfaction, a troubled joy, an aching absence, an expectant hope, or a host of other feelings. We look forward to pleasures. We can be moved to tears at our national anthem. We are satisfied or joyous when our devotion to our cause helps achieve its goals. We hope that the aching absence of desolation—discussed with regard to Mother Teresa in Chapter 5—will abate. To have faith without feeling or emotions would be like loving a person to whom one had no emotional response. This is simply not possible.

If we love another, we act for his or her benefit. We may merely wish the other well, or we may sacrifice our life, our fortune, and our sacred honor so that the other may thrive. We feel regret if our actions harm the person, frustration if our actions fail to help him or her. Love has a volitional or moral component. Fidelity to a lover, care for a child, looking out for a friend's welfare—all of these are acts of love. Cheating on a lover, abusing a child, defrauding a friend—these are acts that show the absence of love. We have expectations about how one who claims to love another should and should not act.

And so with faith. Faith is not reducible to morality, nor is morality reducible to faith. But our faith correlates with who the others are that we are to "do unto" as we would wish them to "do unto us." It is a particularly Christian way of putting it, but while deeds or works cannot be faith, our deeds or works may well show what our faith really is.

Consider a person who professes to have faith in pleasure but never seeks it; or who says she has faith in God but never prays; or who claims that he is utterly devoted to his country but refuses any form of national service; or who claims to have faith in human goodness but acts viciously toward others. These actions belie a person's faith claim. Similarly, atheistic humanists' prayerful participation in a church service each Sunday would belie their claims, too. The claim to have faith in a particular god—or the unarticulated faith in a god—carries expectations to engage in certain kinds of acts and to avoid other sorts of acts.

Personal Gods and Energizing Value Sources

Some of the gods people have faith in are personal, some not. The love one has for another person, a "thou," differs from the love one has for a thing, an "it." My love for my parents, my spouse, or my children has a different quality than my love for good wine, my favorite film, or my country. My love for persons is interactive—I talk to them. I may talk *about* the things I love, but rarely, if ever, do I talk *to* those things.

Those who recognize their god or gods as personal talk to each as a "thou." Often that talk is in the form of a prayer. As I can express my love, beg forgiveness, make requests, and show appreciation in what I say to those I love, so I can do to the personal god or gods in whom I have faith. I may express my love *of* and show my appreciation *for* my country, good sex, or piles of money, but I cannot ask those gods for forgiveness or ask them for help or favors (at least not in any way similar to ways I can interact with persons or personal gods).

Whether we are polytheists, henotheists, or universalists of various kinds, we have different kinds of relationships with a god who is a "thou" rather than a god who is an "it." We can be irreducibly committed to and ultimately concerned with both. We can meditate on the significance of our gods, reflect on how best to express our devotion to them, even serve them in various ways. But only gods who are personal can have concern for or commitment to us. Naturalists do not expect commitment to them from humanity because, finally, humanity is either an abstraction or a widely varied collection of people. To put it succinctly, while we can only really talk *of* impersonal gods, we can and often do talk *to* personal gods.

In short, taking faith to be a relationship melds together the partial understandings surveyed in Chapter 1 to point us toward the whole. If we think of faith as a relationship, we can incorporate the misunderstandings of faith, we can recognize the importance of the subjective side of faith, and we can account for the varieties of faith, worship, and abstinence by acknowledging the many gods of faith. The aspects and qualities highlighted by various accounts of faith are all part of accounting for faith but are simply not the whole of the relationship that is faith.

Faith and Freedom

Yet we have not yet broached a key issue: Is the relationship of faith one we are given or one we choose, a gift or a choice? William

James, as the last chapter noted, construed faith as a free choice. Since his description of the "genuine option situation" shows that one can and must base one's choice on hope or on emotion if one were in such a situation, it presumes that faith is a choice—specifically a choice that one can act on. John Henry Newman echoed the Catholic tradition in assuming that faith is a gift of God to a person. So which is it? Choice or gift?

Again, the analogy of love—in this case romantic love—proves useful. Did one *choose* to fall in love or did one *discover* that one was in love almost as one finds a gift under a Christmas tree? For most of us, neither gift nor choice alone seem an adequate way to describe falling in love. Describing falling in love as the result of a fully free choice neglects the overwhelming amazement and joy that comes over one as one falls in love. Describing falling in love as the result of blind fate, as nonreturnable gift, or as "dumb luck," neglects the seeking and choosing one does, the role one's own mind and heart play in the experience. The problem is that neither choice nor gift seems entirely appropriate. And it is the same with faith.

In some sense, to say that we freely choose our god or gods must be correct, especially for those of us who choose impersonal gods. Impersonal gods cannot give us a gift because gifts require a giver who intends to give us something (leaving out, of course, the sarcastic use of "gift," as when we call a contagious disease a "gift that keeps on giving"). Even those of us who belong to highly structured religious faith traditions have had to choose to recommit ourselves to the tradition when we are confirmed, or celebrate a bar or bat mitzvah, or otherwise move ceremoniously to maturity in faith. This is simply part of the evolution of our faith. Our "choice" may have been practically forced on us when we were young. But we have to choose as we become more mature whether we will continue to accept the gift. Of course, our "choice" may be so constrained by parents or family or religious community that it is no real self-determination at all. Since such a choice is not in any sense free, it is not of concern here.

Some of us have been on a quest that has led us to reject or rebel against our inherited faith and to make a different commitment, for example, to secular humanism. Nonetheless, it seems not entirely right to say that our new faith was our choice *alone*. For surely there was something about that new tradition, about the god it teaches us to relate to, that attracted us, that seemed something like a gift that was already "there" waiting for us to accept it, even if there was no "giver." To take faith as a purely free choice would deny, for instance, the compulsion that drew Stephen Dedalus to his art or Willoughby to his pleasure.

The real question here is not between choice and gift, but between being free or being forced to have faith. If we cannot choose to accept or spurn faith, we are forced to consent to it or to seem to do so. Such a faith is a burden imposed on us. To put it all too simply, if we can choose to accept or spurn faith, we are free. This faith may well be a gift of a god or God. Hence, faith is both gift and choice. True faith is a gift that is freely accepted.

Philosophers have debated the concept of freedom for so long that freedom has become an essentially contested concept. That is, philosophers have basically reached a stalemate about understanding what freedom *really* is. Is it the ability to act or the absence of restraint from acting? Is freedom compatible with causal determinism? Are we really free if we are so strongly influenced that the statistical probability of our acting against that influence is tiny? Making headway on these issues is beyond the scope of this book.

However, we can say that it seems to most of us that we are, at least sometimes, including very important junctures in our lives, free to believe, feel, or act in certain ways—even though we recognize that most of the time we may not have any effective freedom to think, feel, or act other than as we do. It also seems to most of us that we can tell the difference between being forced to think, feel, or act in certain ways and being free not to think, feel, or act those ways. Perhaps most of the time we are not effectively free—we just do what we do, being neither forced nor forbidden, choosing consciously or not; we just do what we do.

The issue of freedom arises pointedly at crucial junctures in our lives—Jamesian "genuine option situations" are possible only if we have freedom. And such situations are crucial. When we are young (at least), we hope or assume that we will neither be forced to marry someone we do not love nor forbidden to marry the one we love. We expect that we are neither forced nor forbidden to vote for the candidate of our choice in an election and to have our ballot counted. We expect that, even if it entails hardships, we will neither be forced nor forbidden to have faith in the god that we come to recognize, or have always recognized, as being the source of meaning and the center of value in our lives. In each of these cases we expect that we are free enough to choose to accept a gift. Even if faith is a gift, we are free at least to consent to living in and living out a faith.

CONCLUSION

In sum, faith is the relationship one has to one's god or gods. It has a rational component—we know what is important, at least, about what we believe in. It has an affective or emotional component—we have joy, love, satisfaction, fulfillment, or hope in this relationship. It has a volitional or moral component—not only does our faith require courage in the faith of risk, but it also leads us to engage in patterns of behavior appropriate to the relationship and to avoid inappropriate behavior. It is this moral component that has given us one clue to understanding the shapes of faith in practice by noting how a pattern of faith treats the "other" invoked in a golden rule. It has a spiritual pattern shown in the ways we worship our gods and how we sacrifice.

But this discussion has had to remain fairly abstract, even with the examples used along the way. We need to consider some expressions of faith to bring this journey in understanding back down to earth and out of the conceptual ether. That's material for Chapter 3.

3

Expressing Faith

To understand faith concretely, we need to analyze sample expressions of faith. One kind of expression is a creed. A creed expresses the tenets of a faith. To analyze expressions of faith is to do theology. Etymologically, *theos* is the Greek word for "god"; *logos* is the Greek word for "word." Theology at its simplest is talking of gods and/or God. Theology can be defined (as Saint Anselm of Canterbury did in the eleventh century) as "faith seeking understanding." And if we all have our god or gods and we are to talk of our god or gods, then we cannot avoid doing theology if we want to understand something about the seas of faith in which we swim.

This chapter first explores the practice of theology and then analyzes four creeds that express the central claims of four streams of faith. Chapter 4 goes on to explore other expressions of faith.

UNDERSTANDING FAITH

Typically, theology is taken to be understanding *our own* faith or faith tradition. Christians generally do Christian theology, Buddhists do Buddhist "theology," and so forth. Here, the concept of theological work is somewhat broader. It includes exploring faith and faith traditions other than our own. We may not be professional theologians or even very reflective about our own lives. Yet we share this challenge to understand faith, even if we do not have or study the same faiths.

This approach implies, odd as it sounds, that there are humanist theologies, secular theologies, and even "atheist" theologies. To be an atheist is to be a non-theist. But one cannot be a non-theist in general. One rejects *particular* deities. When Christianity was in its infancy in the Roman Empire of the first and second centuries, Christians were accused by some Roman authorities of being atheists. Of course Christians were atheists—at least with regard to the Roman gods. But that does not mean they were atheists about *all* gods. Far from it! They had faith in God, revealed especially in and through a Jew from Nazareth named Jesus. As then, so now: one is a believer *with regard to* a particular god or gods and an atheist *with regard to* other particular gods. We are all believers—regarding the god or gods we have faith in. Yet we are all atheists, too—at least regarding the gods we don't have faith in. So, we are all forced to do theology, to understand faith.

Understanding Faith and Faiths

Theology is a discipline that seeks to understand ourselves, the world in which we live, and the god or gods that we worship. Some of us are quite aware of our faith. Others of us are not. Some of us are aware of the god(s) we have faith in and the myths that structure our worlds. For others, faith remains relatively unexamined. One task of theology is making explicit our relationship to the object(s) of our faith.

One does not have to be religious to do theology. One simply has to seek understanding of the relationship we call faith. One may seek to understand one's own faith or another's. One may want to study another faith to clarify one's own. But whatever the purpose, whatever the faith we bring to the exploration, whatever faith we study, we are talking about god. We are doing theology.

Theology is similar to the academic study of religion. It uses the same methods. It studies many of the same people and communities. The differences are that theology studies not only religious traditions and the people whose faith they shape, but all who have faith, religious or not. Theology also focuses on the particular relationship one has to one's god, whether a personal god or an impersonal or abstract ideal.

Expressing One's Faith in Public

Many of us think that expressing our faith is too personal to be proper in public. We may be uncomfortable with any government support of "faith-based initiatives." We may feel that displaying symbols of faith like a crucifix or a Star of David on public property is inappropriate. Yet even if our faith should be little seen and less heard in public, our personal faith is possible only because of the public character of the language we speak. We can never isolate our faith to the private sphere of our interiority alone.

For me to say—even to myself alone—what I have faith in, I must be able to use a language that I have learned. To express my most private thoughts requires a public, shared language. I may intend to use words *literally* or *metaphorically* or *symbolically*. My speaking or writing may be awkward, hesitant, or unfocused; it may be poetic, prosaic, elegant, quick, or precise. But the language I use to express even my most private ideas is necessarily public. I cannot say even to myself, "I have faith in woofy," unless I can say, however indirectly or metaphorically or poetically, what "woofy" is and what "woofy" means to me. To express my faith— or any of my ideas—I have to use a language that I have learned with and from others.

All too often religious people or their opponents claim that faith is subjective. This is true, though only partially true. Simply because *I* have a faith does not make it only subjective. My relationship with my beloved may be personal, but it is not only subjective. And I can talk about it with her or about her with you only because we share a language. As in love, so in faith. We have to use a public language to say anything at all about either of them. I cannot talk of my faith without talking of the god(s) I have faith in. Even "subjective" faith is a relationship to an object of that faith.

Just as my relationship with my beloved deepens as we grow in understanding, so our faith in our god(s) can deepen as we grow in understanding our faith. As we grow in understanding, we do theology. We understand our faith or that of others by understanding expressions of faith. But where do we start? Perhaps the most obvious place is with the brief statements formulated to express the beliefs central to a faith—creeds.

ARTICULATING FAITH

A creed is a brief summary statement that displays the shape of one's faith. When we are asked what we believe in, we may articulate that faith in a creed. A creed may be an official one that is recognized by a community, such as the Nicene Creed in most forms of Christianity. Or a creed may be one's own distinctive summary of one's particular faith.

Not all creeds are comprehensive. My creed may take no specific stance on issues that you find important components of your own faith statement. Hence, creeds may not be comparable as wholes.

Nonetheless, creeds can be compared and evaluated with regard to a particular topic if they make claims about that topic. For example, most formal creeds say something about what it means to be a flourishing human or what humans' ultimate goals are or ought to be. Hence, we can compare creeds with regard to their anthropologies, their views of human nature and human destiny, if they make anthropological claims.

In this section we reflect on articulations of four different faiths. We explore a contemporary summary of secular humanism, draw a summary of Christian faith from Christianity's greatest theologian, analyze a faith attributed to many young Americans by a theologically savvy sociologist, and explore a classic summary found in Mahayana Buddhist traditions. In each case what follows is *not* the last word on these faiths but rather an introduction to their basic shapes.

The Humanist Manifesto

Humanism is faith in humanity. The American Humanist Association has issued three versions of the manifesto over the years as a way of summarizing the tenets of humanism. It functions as a loose creed to guide humanists and those who want to understand what humanism stands for. As the association notes, not all humanists would subscribe to every statement in the manifesto. There is no orthodox humanism to which all humanists subscribe, and no "orthodoxy police." Nonetheless, the manifesto provides a touchstone for understanding the beliefs of secular humanism.

As the current version of the manifesto puts it, "Humanism is a progressive philosophy of life that, without supernaturalism, affirms our ability and responsibility to lead ethical lives of personal fulfillment that aspire to the greater good of humanity." Our personal fulfillment, the manifesto states later, "emerges from individual participation in the service of humane ideals." Humanity is the energizing center of value and source of meaning for humanists. Humanity is the god of humanism.

The manifesto rejects "supernaturalism." That is, humanists find no good reason to think that there is a creator of the universe who is in some way outside of the universe that science explores. Nor do humanists find reason to believe that there is any human life beyond this one—in contrast to Christian belief in heaven (and hell) or Hindu belief in reincarnation. Without the threat or promise of an afterlife, living morally in our time and our place must be not only personally satisfying, but also good for all. Being a good person does not *merit* any reward; it is its own reward.

Humanism has a fundamental vision of a satisfying human life. "Humanism—guided by reason, inspired by compassion, and informed by experience—encourages us to live life well and fully." Part of this vision is trust in science: "Knowledge of the world is derived by observation, experimentation, and rational analysis." Human beings are natural beings. We are "an integral part of nature, the result of unguided evolutionary change. Humanists recognize nature as self-existing." Rejecting both a supernatural soul that makes humans something more than natural and an intelligent force that guides evolution, traditional *religious* values have little or no place in the faith of humanists. Hence, the appellation *secular* humanism.

Humanists see ethical principles as based in "human need and interest as tested by experience." Humanists' concerns are not limited to human welfare and human needs but extend "to the global ecosystem and beyond." In recognizing humanity as a child of nature, humanists' concerns must extend to Mother Nature as well as humanity abstracted from nature. Indeed, humanists find that perspectives that treat human values as separate from the natural world are misleading.

While affirming the inherent worth and dignity of each individual, the manifesto also affirms that humans "are social by nature and find meaning in relationships. . . . Working to benefit society maximizes individual happiness." This intrinsic connection between the individual and the community differentiates humanism from the forms of hedonism, egoism, and narcissism discussed in the previous chapter. Secular humanists tend to presume that democracy is a form of government that expresses humanist ideals better than other forms. But particular humanists may fall almost anywhere between the poles of radical individualism and radical communalism as the best expressions of human equality.

The manifesto affirms commitment to diversity and to "respect those of differing yet humane views"; to an open, democratic, secular society; and to "human rights and civil liberties." Humanists find it "a civic duty to participate in the democratic process and a planetary duty to protect nature's integrity, diversity, and beauty in a secure, sustainable manner." Secular humanism is a faith whose expression is necessarily political. While certainly not rejecting charity, humanists are committed to working to structure or restructure human society in a humane, more just, way.

Humanity is able "to progress toward its highest ideals. The responsibility for our lives and the kind of world in which we live is ours and ours alone." We are responsible for what happens in the world. While we attribute much of the suffering in the world to natural causes ranging from birth defects and cancer to earthquakes, tsunamis, and hurricanes, we are responsible for working to overcome both the causes of individual suffering and the social causes that build human communities that cannot resist and endure well the natural disasters that afflict them.

Religious people often vilify secular humanism. Yet many religious people could affirm the personal and social values articulated in the manifesto. Most religious people would find the opposition to supernaturalism wrong-headed and the account of the sources of suffering and the hope for progress also too little inflected by a consciousness of human sinfulness. Moreover, most humanists acknowledge that many religious traditions provided earlier formulations of and motivations for holding the values that humanists hold dear. While there are real disagreements, religious people who heap abuse on humanism ignore the fact that religious people and secular humanists share many concrete values.

The *Enchiridion* of Saint Augustine of Hippo

The second creed we consider is drawn from a handbook of the Christian faith prepared by Saint Augustine of Hippo for the use of a layperson early in the fifth century. Written long before the split between Western Roman Catholic Christianity and the Eastern Orthodox churches in the eleventh century or the Protestant-Catholic split in the sixteenth century, it provides a statement of the fundamentals of the Christian faith untainted by later polemics. In this little book Augustine sought "to state what must be believed, what must be hoped, what must be loved" by Christians.

Augustine's intellectual edifice is built on the pillars of a traditional Christian story of the world: creation, fall, incarnation, redemption, resurrection.

First, Augustine claims that all that is, is good. Everything that exists is good because it was created by God, who is all good and all powerful. This raises the obvious question: If God made everything good, why do so many bad things happen? To account for the evil in the world, Augustine claims that evil is the privation of good. Note that evil is not merely the absence of good. Rather, when anything that exists is not what it should be, that is an evil state of affairs. An engine that is out of tune, an ecology that is out of balance, a tumor consisting of cells growing out of control, a person afflicted with psychological illness, or an unjust society is not what it should be. These are evils because something has deprived them of being what they are supposed to be.

But where does that privation come from? Augustine's second point is to note that evil must somehow originate from entities that are good. But how can good entities produce evil? His hypothesis is that evil originates from a fall. Naturally good, but changeable, the wills of angels and humans fall short of willing the unchangeable, perfect good. Since everything in the world is good, but only God is perfectly good, what is in the world is imperfectly good. This imperfection led (not inevitably, but really) to sin.

The result of choosing less than one's true good is a warping and twisting of one's very nature or essence. Many Christians conceive this defect as original sin—a tendency to do evil that all human beings inherit. Though God created us good, humanity, in the first human, Adam, fell into sin. And all human beings ever since have inherited that sin as if it were a genetic defect. God may have created humanity good, but in the wake of this first sin, every human being born falls short of that original goodness.

Hence, human beings, for all the good they are and do, are also weak in the face of temptation, ignorant in various ways, and beset by desires for what is not good for them. These defects that all people share have consequences: all the evils that afflict humanity, both individually and socially.

The world is full of great evils. All of us are so warped by "original sin" that we are inclined to sin and harm from our very beginning. And not only are we inclined to sin, we are awash in the effects wreaked on us by our own sins and the sins of others. The human race is a mass of sin, damned to suffer and to die as a result of sin.

Third, there is good news: God has entered the world, becoming human in Jesus of Nazareth. God-with-us has saved us from sin, suffering, and death; Jesus Christ, truly human and truly divine, accepted death on a cross so that we might truly live. This is redemption. It is not merely "going to heaven when one dies," although that is a crucial part of the story. It is the gracious healing of human nature, replacing in each of us the good of which we were deprived. Those who accept salvation and live in the realization of the love of God know that they are or will be saved from the evils that beset them. Yes, each may be afflicted by multiple forms of suffering, but the healing of mind, heart, and will that constitutes salvation leads one to be and do good.

This good work can be variously described. I would say that it means that one will work to understand what is wrong, be motivated to repair the evils in the world, and choose to work to contribute to restoring what is good for creatures deprived of their full goodness. Augustine would have called this charity, a form of love. Today we can adapt this working for good in light of our present understandings of the evils that afflict us. We will be motivated to learn how to work for goods like sustainable energy sources, a healthy ecosystem, care for the sick and dying, cures for physical and psychological illnesses, and a just society. One will choose to do so and to have the confidence that God will support the human good now and forever—for Augustine believed that all people would be resurrected, "us" to glory and "them" (if there are any people who are not part of "us"—a point on which Augustine seems unclear) to ruin.

As the Humanist Manifesto merely maps the main tenets of the faith of humanism rather than displaying everything humanists find important, so this summary of Augustine's *Enchiridion* merely displays the pillars of the Christian faith, not its whole architecture. As some humanists would not accept every claim of the manifesto as stated, some Christians would not accept every one of Augustine's points (or even this interpretation of Augustine's *Enchiridion*). Nonetheless, it should be clear that both faiths support the intellectual, moral, and emotional goods that humans display and reject what is personally and socially evil. They disagree, of course, on the source of good and the overcoming of evil. The Christian finds God the source of all good, and all creation good because it is from God, even if creation in general and humans in particular are deformed by sin. The humanist finds humanity the source of good; the universe just is what it is—neither good nor evil. And while the Christian and the humanist can agree on many, if not all, of the active principles for overcoming evil, they agree neither on the sources of good or of evil nor the possibility of ultimate resolution in an eternal life freely given us by the love of God.

Moralistic Therapeutic Deism

In an influential study published in 2005, *Soul Searching: The Religious and Spiritual Lives of American Teenagers*, Christian Smith and Melinda Lundquist Denton claimed that "moralistic, therapeutic deism" (MTD) was the real faith of the typical American teenager. And, many would argue, the real faith of many

Americans who think they are staunch Christians. Smith and Denton engaged in extensive sociological research to construct MTD. Perhaps more than any other "faith tradition," MTD shows that the sea of faith in the United States has many currents that can be amalgamated.

Smith and Denton formulated the creed of MTD as follows:

- A God exists who created and ordered the world and watches over human life on earth.
- God wants people to be good, nice, and fair to one another, as taught in the Bible and by most world religions.
- The central goal of life is to be happy and to feel good about oneself.
- God does not need to be particularly involved in one's life except when God is needed to resolve a problem.
- Good people go to heaven when they die.

Smith and Denton commented: "God is something like a combination Divine Butler and Cosmic Therapist: he is always on call, takes care of any problems that arise, professionally helps his people to feel better about themselves, and does not become too personally involved in the process."

Many have commented on the self-centered goal of life, the lack of a sense of the seriousness of sin and evil, and the lack of any need to act for the good of others in MTD (in contrast to both the classic Christian tradition articulated by Augustine and the tenets of humanism). Yet, many traditional Christians would agree with all but the third and fourth of the summary statements above. I have trouble imagining serious secular humanists agreeing with any of the propositions. If anyone actually holds this faith, that person has swallowed bits and pieces from the many streams of self-help, optimism, narcissism, entitlement, and comforting deism that flow through our culture.

This adolescent religiosity has resonances with the narcissism discussed in Chapter 2—it seems very self-centered. Yet adolescence is an unstable time. Traveling from a childhood they want to abandon to an adulthood they do not know how to embrace, adolescents in U.S. culture live in a time of uncertainty, rebellion, struggle, and searching between naive and mature forms of faith. It remains to be seen whether MTD is merely a phase on a journey or will endure as a live option for adults.

The picture of humanity that emerges in MTD is that of a dependent patient entitled to be healthy, both now and forever. The conflicts and evils in the world, recognized in most faith traditions, are minimized. God is invoked to ensure that entitlement to self-realization. The lack of serious moral components in MTD suggests that this faith requires no moral commitments other than "being nice."

If MTD is a spirituality, it seems to ignore the need for any sacrifice. Being fair to others, for example, may require sacrificing one's own comfort in particular ways. While MTD may echo notes of contemporary popular Christianity, it fits more with the polytheistic faith of the Roman Empire than the monotheism of classic Christianity. MTD finds the Cosmic Butler worthy of worship when one has needs. Otherwise, that God is not the center of one's life. Hence, it is not clear that MTD is a relationship with an irreducible center of meaning and source of value.

The Three Jewels of Buddhism

Reciting the Three Jewels is chanting or praying or repeating a mantra. *Which* of those acts one is performing in uttering those words and what those words mean varies among the various Buddhist traditions. But to invoke the Three Jewels by saying "I take refuge in the Buddha, I take refuge in the dharma, I take refuge in the samgha" is to declare oneself a Buddhist.

Buddha is the first Jewel. Buddha is not only the man, Gautama Siddhartha, a prince who lived some twenty-six centuries ago in India. Gautama was the first to teach the way that became called Buddhism. But *Buddha* also designates anyone who has reached full human development, that is Enlightenment, after many lifetimes of striving.

For Theravada Buddhists, Gautama was a teacher to be followed. He was an *arhat*, a person who reached Enlightenment and entered Nirvana. For Mahayana Buddhists, Gautama is an exemplary *boddhisattva*, an Enlightened person of perfect compassion who could attain Nirvana on death but vows to accept Nirvana only when all sentient beings do. For some Mahayana Buddhists, Buddha is more a divine savior than an exemplar. However one construes Buddha, to take refuge in Buddha is to give oneself to and to seek guidance from Buddha.

Buddha is not a "soul" with multiple "bodily" reincarnations. Gautama reacted to the classic Hindu doctrine that what seems to be my individual soul or your individual soul *(atman)* is really a manifestation of the "Soul" at the heart of all there is (Brahman). In contrast, Buddha taught an *anatta* or "no soul" doctrine. The "self" or "soul" or enduring "I" is an illusion. What passes from one life to the next is not a soul but something more like energy flowing in a certain direction, like a flame passed from dying candle to fresh candle, not some spiritual "thing." To come to Nirvana is to realize fully that the self is an illusion; it is to stop the unceasing round of energy transmitted over and over and over; it is to come to peace. One could say that the *anatta* doctrine swims against the monistic current of the classic Hindu traditions.

The dharma is both the way things are and what the Buddha Gautama taught—fundamentally, the Four Noble Truths. The first truth is the description of life: life is suffering. All beings suffer from not having what they crave and not craving what they have. This does not mean we are sad or in pain all the time. Rather, it means that we cannot escape a nagging discontent with who we are and what we have. (Of course, the oppressed and the elite suffer in different ways, but we all are discontented). The second truth is the diagnosis: suffering comes from craving. If I crave knowledge, I suffer because I do not have it; if I crave to be free of burdens, I suffer because I cannot but bear them. We all crave things or crave to be better than we are right now. This craving is the cause of suffering. The third truth follows logically. It is the prescription: to stop suffering, stop craving. The fourth truth is the therapy: we are to walk the Eightfold Path, the practices that end suffering. The ending of suffering is Nirvana—a state we may taste when we can just live in the moment as it is. But those moments pass, and we return to craving and suffering. Fully realizing

Nirvana is the final extinction of the flame of desire and the advent of eternal peace.

The Eightfold Path is arranged more logically than sequentially. As with all skills, from bicycling to ballet, one begins at a very basic level. By working at each practice, however inexpertly, one comes to improve in all of them. The path begins with *right understanding* of the Buddha-dharma, especially realizing the *anatta* doctrine as true of oneself. *Right thought* involves being clear on one's purpose in life and in one's perception of and reflection on reality. *Right speech* not only means speaking without deceiving but also involves speaking gently and kindly. *Right action* includes avoiding killing, sexual immorality, stealing, lying, and intoxicants. *Right livelihood* involves not only what one does to support oneself but how one conducts one's business—in line with right action. *Right effort* weeds out bad thoughts and desires of every kind that may come to us, often despite our best intentions. *Right mindfulness* prescribes what to think about when meditating. *Right concentration* prescribes how to develop one's ability to focus in meditation. It is absorption in meditation that brings peace, a taste of Nirvana—and when perfect, one comes to ultimate peace. There is, of course, much else attributed to the Buddha's teaching, but this is the heart of the dharma.

The samgha (or sangha) is the community of the Buddhist tradition, the assembly of those who live in and live out the tradition. In some areas it has a narrower meaning and encompasses the communities of monks and/or nuns. In others it includes laymen and laywomen as well. To take refuge in the samgha is to realize that we are not alone in this journey. Each of us has an uncountable number of fellow travelers who can guide and support us—and also an uncountable number of others that we are to guide and support.

Each of the Buddhist traditions has different organizational forms and many other practices and doctrines. Nonetheless, the Three Jewels are at the heart of all the Buddhist traditions, just as the Humanist Manifesto articulates the center of secular humanist traditions and the *Enchiridion* displays the fundamental pillars of the Christian tradition.

A Brief Comparison of the Four Creeds

Each creed has an anthropology, a view of what it means to be human. The humanist sees individuals and the human community as a "work in progress." Suffering is as much a part of life as joy is, evil as much a part of the way things are as good is. We can work both individually and together to ameliorate that suffering. In the concluding paragraph of "The Free Man's Worship" (1903), written by one of the great secular humanists of the twentieth century, Bertrand Russell, the anthropology of secular humanism is shown (in a rather pessimistic key):

> Brief and powerless is man's life; on him and all his race the slow, sure doom falls pitiless and dark. Blind to good and evil, reckless of destruction, omnipotent matter rolls on its relentless way; for man, condemned today to lose his dearest, tomorrow himself to pass through the gate of darkness, it remains only to cherish, ere yet the blow fall, the lofty thoughts that ennoble his little day; disdaining the coward terrors of the slave of Fate, to worship at the shrine that his own hands have built; undismayed by the empire of chance, to preserve a mind free from the wanton tyranny that rules his outward life; proudly defiant of the irresistible forces that tolerate, for a moment, his knowledge and his condemnation, to sustain alone, a weary but unyielding Atlas, the world that his own ideals have fashioned despite the trampling march of unconscious power.

The anthropology of secular humanism has moral implications as well. Because each of us is, as Russell put it earlier in the same essay, "united with his fellow-men, by the strongest of all ties, the tie of a common doom, the free man finds that a new vision is with him always, shedding over every daily task the light of love." That love involves sympathy, affection, encouragement, and meeting the needs of others regardless of their strengths or weaknesses. We are to live both with and for our fellows, because ultimately nothing will remain of our achievements save what they carry forward after our inevitable death. Since there is nothing beyond the grave, our only reward is the satisfaction we get from being and doing our best.

In one sense secular humanism seems a pessimistic faith. But the humanist would say that it is realistic. It is a faith that eschews wishful thinking. Buddhism is often said to be a pessimistic faith. But Buddhists would claim that their faith, like that of humanism, is realistic about the present. The Buddhist traditions also explain just how we got where we are (as humanism cannot) and offer hope for the future.

First, the Buddhist traditions find that each of us is born in the circumstances that we deserve, based on the actions of our previous lives. In this life, or the next, each pays the price for one's evil deeds or reaps the rewards for one's good deeds. One is responsible for one's actions. Hence, I am responsible for being born into the circumstances that shape my current life because those circumstances were determined by my actions in my previous lives. And in this life I am also responsible for creating the circumstances of my next life. This is realistic—presuming I accept the doctrine of rebirth.

Second, the Buddhist traditions recognize the reality of suffering. But the traditions offer paths out of that suffering world, the eternal round of life and death, and into the still peace of Nirvana, the end of suffering. Since I have no soul, I will not and cannot "exist" in Nirvana. For those of us enslaved by the illusion that we are individual enduring selves, this may sound pessimistic. But in the face of a realistic understanding of suffering and death similar in some ways to secular humanism, Buddhist faith incorporates hope as a secular humanistic faith cannot. Buddhist faith holds out very different sort of hope in comparison with Christian traditions.

Various streams of hope shape the traditions. In Jodo-Shinshu, a Japanese form of Buddhism, the Buddha is seen as a savior. To have and proclaim one's faith in and love for Amidha Buddha ensures ultimate salvation. In Theravada traditions an individual engages in the practices that Buddha taught until the individual reaches the deathlessness of Nirvana. I may not reach Nirvana in this life, but there is hope for me in a future life—and I am responsible for the circumstances into which I will be reborn.

The Christian conviction that humanity is created good but that humans are born sinners is a blend of pessimism and hope. Christians believe that only God's grace, God's initiative, can ultimately save people from sin, suffering, and death. Human beings can do nothing for themselves without God's grace. In this way Christianity is pessimistic—sin has so badly warped God's good creation of humanity that individuals can do nothing to save themselves.

Christianity also seems to include an optimism expressed in the hope for salvation. That optimism is expressed in many ways, not the least of which is working to improve the world just because God is glorified when people thrive. Even if only God saves people ultimately, in the proximate conditions of this life Christians can and should work to ameliorate suffering. Without such work the hope of Christians remains an empty slogan.

Christians disagree about whom God saves. Some think God may save some people, those who believe in God through Jesus Christ; others think God may save each human being at the end of the single life God has given him or her. But most Christians agree that humans cannot save themselves. Humanity was created good, turned to sin, but can be saved from sin and its effects by God.

In contrast, a Theravadin Buddhist thinks that all sentient beings may come to Nirvana, even though they experience many rebirths, lives, and deaths. A secular humanist thinks that people can and should work to overcome suffering but that nothing can save them from the obliteration of death at the end of the one life they have. In sum, all three traditions agree that humans are to work for what is good, even though they may well disagree on what that good is, why we have an ability to work for it, how to discover it, and what results from such work.

Each of these traditions can be viewed as a school for faith—a point implied in the previous chapters and made explicit here. In narrating the creed, in telling the stories, in using the symbols, in learning how to practice a faith, those who are mature in the faith tradition literally school others who are learners or novices. The Christian church, the American Humanist Association, the Buddhist samgha—all of these are not merely associations but rather schools that can teach one how to see, how to feel, how to act, how to worship, how to abstain. The people who live in and live out a faith tradition form a school for faith. (It is unclear to me how MTD could be the tenets of a school for faith; in that sense, if MTD is a real faith, it seems parasitic on the streams of faith in the culture).

In many ways individuals may be "self taught," that is, shape their individual faith in their own ways. They may be schooled in no particular community of faith. But, more commonly, we learn from *many* currents of faith in a pluralistic society. Christians, humanists, misers, nationalists—all may school us in various ways. Individuals then use what they have learned to shape their own faiths.

Whether one's faith is unique or whether the tenets of one's faith conform closely to a "school" of faith, our pluralistic culture makes it inevitable that we are not schooled in only one tradition. We swim not in one homogenous sea of faith but in a sea that comprises many currents of faith. How we organize or order what we learn from these varied streams determines in large part the shape of our faith—from narcissistic to universalist. But more of that in the next chapter.

CONCLUSION

Considered abstractly—that is, considered in abstraction from the other expressions of faith—the meaning of a creed is vague. The question that remains is more concrete: how is a creed related to the stories we tell, the symbols we use, and the practices in which we engage? In Chapter 4 we continue exploring the streams of faith, showing how the real significance of creedal statements is shown by these expressions of living faith.

4

Living Faith

How does one live out the faith one professes in a creed? This chapter seeks to understand three practical components in which we express our faith. If creeds sketch the tenets of faith, *stories* flesh out those sketches, *symbols* crystalize faith in images, and *practices* school one in how to live in and live out the faith. Stories, symbols, and practices can also focus faith concretely and can evoke cascades of meaning.

Professing creeds, telling stories, and using symbols are all practices of faith. But they are contextualized by a host of other practices that show how to live in and live out a faith tradition. The final section of the chapter focuses on the significance of other practices for the life of faith. In effect, we first do narrative theology, then symbolic theology, and then practical theology in order to exemplify and explore how one lives one's faith and how one is schooled in how to worship and what may need to be sacrificed.

STORIES OF FAITH

The creeds we examined briefly in the previous chapter are abstractions from stories, symbols, and practices. Creeds can be used as rules that guide a person in understanding how to express one's faith. Members of faith traditions can use a creed to guide the present understanding and future development of the tradition. But creeds are not to be equated with a faith. Rather, they are a summary of the tenets of a faith. One of the reasons that moralistic therapeutic deism may not be a creed at all is that it hardly seems a set of rules to guide one in understanding a faith that can endure beyond adolescence.

Most Christians, for example, take the confession or creed of the Council of Chalcedon (451 c.e.) as a rule to guide them in talking about Jesus Christ. The creed asserts that he is truly human and truly divine, one person with both a human nature and the divine nature. The council ruled out stories that portray Jesus as merely human or only divine (in human disguise). The Humanist Manifesto provides another example. It rules out universe stories that tell of an intelligent designer who stands somehow "behind" the universe and who can be discerned, at least dimly, by reflection on evidence in the universe. Creeds function as both positive and negative guides for expressing one's faith.

Narratives contribute substantially to communicating and expressing what one's faith means. People tell stories to understand the world they inhabit and to show themselves and others ways of navigating in that world. Creeds tend to be abstractions—they have a timeless quality. Stories, on the other hand, are always set in particular (sometimes paradigmatic or archetypal) times and places.

This section lays out the types or genres of stories of faith. As this is not a treatise in literary analysis but an essay on the shape of faith, the categories will not map perfectly on those common in literary theory. But that should not be surprising, as each approach has a different purpose. Theirs is to analyze texts. Ours is to explore the currents of faith. Theirs is to engage in literary criticism. Ours is to engage in narrative theology, that is, to understand how stories flesh out the shape of faith.

Myths

In popular parlance, *myth* is a term often used to denote a false or misleading tale. It is a term of disparagement. That is *not* the way we use the term in the study of faith traditions. Here, *myth* is a technical term used to define a certain narrative genre and to distinguish this genre from other narrative genres important for understanding how people use stories to express their faith.

A myth is *a story that sets up a world*. The most obvious myths are the myths of the beginning of the universe. One is the creation of the world by God in the book of Genesis. Other myths can be developed out of the scientific theory of the "initial singularity," a.k.a. the "Big Bang." Science cannot penetrate beyond or behind this singularity because there is no evidence available from a time "earlier" than that. But to assert that there was nothing before the Big Bang, or that we live in one phase of an eternal oscillation of Big Bangs and Big Crunches, or to claim that a Cosmic Designer "fine tuned the Big Bang" to create the conditions for life is to create a myth. Each of these stories "sets up" a world in which most of us live. But the worlds these myths set up are as different as are the worlds of the Humanist Manifesto and the *Enchiridion* of Augustine.

No one lives without a myth, either implicit or explicit. We may think that the world is senseless or meaningless or empty. We may think that myths are for the mindless or the childish or the weak. But implicit in this anti-mythical view is a myth of the world, perhaps the myth of Social Darwinism that accepts the creed of secular humanism discussed in Chapter 3, but incorporates it in a myth that only the socially and physically fit members of a society are fully human and do, or should be allowed to, survive and reproduce. If one lives in a world, one has a myth. The alternative is the flashing, booming confusion of unabated chaos.

The rejection of all myth is itself a myth. People who say they reject myth reject specific myths. In rejecting those myths, they set up a world that fits a different kind of faith, a nonreligious faith. Such a story of the universe may include a powerful nonreligious or antireligious pillar, a robust assertion of the sufficiency of science or common sense to display the real world, and an understanding of the world and perhaps even human life as fundamentally meaningless. But such a story is still a myth.

Myths cannot be evaluated as either true or false in any direct way. There are no standards beyond myths to measure them because myths are the fundamental stories that articulate the contours of the world we inhabit. Sometimes people treat scientific myths as criteria for evaluating religious myths. While religious traditions need to take account of scientific research if they are not to be fixed illusions, to privilege one myth as a criterion for assessing all others is arbitrary.

Myths are not "lenses" on some world that exists independent of myth. Myths express what the world is. A world independent of myth is either uninhabited or incomprehensible. Every world with humans in it is inhabited. And any world without humans in it has no humans to understand it. But we do inhabit our world, so there is no "world-independent-of-our-concepts-of-it" over against which we can measure a myth. There are no purely myth-independent criteria by which to judge myths. Nonetheless, there are principles that most, if not all of us, use in the practice of assessing faith and faiths. Chapter 5 explores how to evaluate myths and other stories of faith.

Typically, a myth portrays the origin and destiny of the universe and of humanity. Ancient myths focus on a "time before time" and a "place we cannot replace." They are nonscientific. The stories in modern myths have to cope with the universe that science has revealed to us. Both ancient and modern myths show in the most general terms why the world is the way it is. They usually also say or show why good and evil are distributed as they are in the world.

To accept a myth is to accept it as expressing a fundamental truth about the world. But this truth is not the sort one can test on a true-false quiz in class. (Consider the silliness of "T or F: God created the world." "T or F: Humans are the result of unguided evolution.") The truth of a myth is different from whether a particular assertion or claim is true or false.

The truth of a myth is a *constitutive* truth. A constitution sets the rules by which we judge whether particular laws or actions are appropriate or inappropriate, constitutional or unconstitutional. Lawyers in a criminal trial, for example, debate whether a particular search violated a defendant's constitutional rights. Some laws passed by Congress and approved by the president are challenged in court for their constitutionality. Analogously, a myth sets the rules by which we judge whether particular claims are true or false. If we live in a world set up by the Big Bang myth, we must judge as false a claim that the book of Genesis is literally true. If we live in a world set up by a "fundamentalist" reading of the Genesis myth, we have to conclude that scientific accounts of evolution are false theories. We usually assess hypotheses but take our myths and the world they create for granted. We usually deal in the realm of evaluation, of evaluative truth, not in the realm of constitution, or constitutive truth.

Myths are not private or subjective. Yes, they are believed or attacked by individuals, but these stories are not individual property. Their elements are shared and must be communicable to others even if the whole myth is fairly idiosyncratic. Myths are expressed in a shared language, not one impervious to understanding by any person other than the storyteller.

The creation myth in the first chapter of the book of Genesis, for example, portrays the creation of the world by God over a period of six days, with God finding the work of each day good and resting on the seventh day. This Genesis myth is interpreted in a variety of ways. Some read it as descriptively true, that God spent six twenty-four-hour days creating the earth. Others take it as a human representation of the created world as fundamentally good, not as the result of a creation that was initially mixed— good and evil. Some see Genesis as compatible with scientific cosmology when both are properly understood. Others find irreducible opposition between their reading of Genesis and contemporary scientific theories regarding the origin of the physical universe. Jews, Christians, and Muslims all accept the Genesis myth, but in each tradition interpretations vary widely.

Some myths portray the origins and destinies of certain features about the world and humanity. These particular myths may be embedded in more universal myths. For example, the second creation story in the Bible can be read as a myth that portrays the origins of the difficulties in growing crops and the dangers of childbirth (Gn 2:4—3:24). Of course, the story has many other aspects not considered here. The story of the tower of Babel in the Bible (Gn 11:1–9) is a myth that portrays the origins of the diversity of human nations and languages. To put it a bit simply, myths are stories that answer fundamental "why?" questions about things in general or particular aspects of the world and humanity.

Secular humanism also has a myth. It is articulated in multiple forms, but fundamentally it accepts science as the story that sets up the real world. Science is the key to showing the contours of the world. In contrast to the Genesis myth, in the secular humanist myth the world in itself has no meaning or purpose. The final fact about the universe is that the universe just is.

Although the scientific constituents of this myth have changed since Bertrand Russell wrote, we return to his essay of 1903 because it limns the contours of humanist myth clearly:

> Amid such a [purposeless] world, if anywhere, our ideals henceforward must find a home. That man is the product of causes which had no prevision of the end they were achieving; that his origin, his growth, his hopes and fears, his loves and his beliefs, are but the outcome of accidental collocations of atoms; that no fire, no heroism, no intensity of thought and feeling can preserve an individual life beyond the grave; that all the labors of the ages, all the devotion, all the inspiration, all the noonday brightness of human genius, are destined to extinction in the vast death of the solar system, and that the whole temple of man's achievements must inevitably be buried beneath the debris of a universe in ruins—all these things, if not quite beyond dispute, are yet so nearly certain that no philosophy which rejects them can hope to stand. Only within the scaffolding of these truths, only on the firm foundation of unyielding despair, can the soul's habitation henceforth be safely built.

Russell's "scaffolding of these truths" shows the constitutive truths that this myth sets up as the world of secular, scientific humanism.

It is within the context of this myth that the ideals of secular humanism make sense. The Humanist Manifesto is a creed that articulates the scaffolding of this myth in a brief set of statements. The story could be told in many ways—some much more detailed, complex, and scientifically precise than Russell's articulation. But when we take the world as presented by science as the whole real world in which we live, the story science tells is a myth.

Obviously, it makes a difference which myth we accept, which world we live in. Even if myths cannot be directly assessed, there are standards for assessing expressions of faith, including myths. As noted before, we consider assessment in Chapter 5. Here, we simply want to state clearly that stories of faith have different genres and that stories in each of these genres may not be told with the same purposes.

Sagas

Sagas are *stories that give communities their identity.* Not all sagas are expressions of faith. Some are ethnic or familial sagas, such as Alex Haley's *Roots.* Some are national. The notion of Manifest Destiny, that God has ordained that the United States is to expand and conquer the continent to the Pacific Ocean, is a saga. American exceptionalism is a saga about the unique development of the United States as a nation in contrast to other nations in terms of its origins in a free compact of immigrants, its democratic political institutions, and its separation of church and state. But many sagas—even those that seem ethnic, national, or familial—can function much in the same way as myths do. They can express one's faith and shape one's world, even if they are not accounts of the ultimate origin or final destiny of all humanity or the world.

Perhaps the most famous saga of all is the saga of the Exodus. One famous interpretation of this saga is *The Ten Commandments* (1956), an extravagant film produced and directed by Cecil B. DeMille. It is shown regularly on U.S. television, often around Passover and Easter. The plot is that the Hebrews are oppressed as slaves in Egypt. God then raises up a leader, Moses, who challenges the authority of the Egyptian rulers; engages his god, YHWH, in competitions with the gods of the Egyptian priests; calls a series of plagues onto the Egyptians; and then leads the Hebrews out of Egypt toward a land that their god has promised them. The Egyptian leadership sends armed chariots after them. The Hebrews cross the Red Sea on foot, but the Egyptians following them are drowned in the sea by YHWH's command. The Hebrews wander in the desert for forty years. Sometimes they are faithful to their god, sometimes not. During this period they receive the Ten Commandments from YHWH, who gives them to

Moses (a spectacular scene in the movie); Moses also dies, having gazed upon the promised land from a mountain. The Hebrews then fight for the promised land and conquer the inhabitants, the Canaanites. The saga is a story of YHWH's leading the chosen people out of the bondage of slavery into a land that God has promised them.

This saga is a narrative that has encoded the hope for freedom of many. Zionism, for example, developed in Europe in the nineteenth century. It envisioned the reestablishment of a homeland for the Jewish people in the territory of ancient Israel. The establishment of the State of Israel in 1948 was deemed by some Zionists as the beginning of the redemption of the promise of YHWH to Jews that they would have their own land.

The Exodus imagery is also frequently used in Christian liberation theology written from the vantage point of the oppressed. The civil rights movement among African Americans owed much to the motifs of the Exodus saga. Martin Luther King, Jr., invoked Exodus motifs in many of his sermons. Speaking the night before he died, he noted some assassination threats directed against him and then invoked the saga in his conclusion:

> Well, I don't know what will happen now. We've got some difficult days ahead. But it really doesn't matter with me now, because I've been to the mountaintop.
>
> And I don't mind.
>
> Like anybody, I would like to live a long life. Longevity has its place. But I'm not concerned about that now. I just want to do God's will. And He's allowed me to go up to the mountain. And I've looked over. And I've seen the promised land. I may not get there with you. But I want you to know tonight, that we, as a people, will get to the promised land!

The Exodus saga provides both a template for understanding the trials an oppressed people undergo and a reason for hope no matter how bleak the circumstances. Like all sagas, it helps a particular community understand who it is in the greater world that may not be of its making or to its liking.

Action Stories

Action stories are *biographical stories set within a world.* Unlike sagas and myths, action stories do not establish a world or an ethnic or religious community. Rather, they flesh out how we can and should (or should not) live within the world articulated in myth or saga. They school us in how to live a faith.

Action stories may be factual or fictional. Their function is to show what attitudes we are to have, what choices we should make, or what actions we ought perform. Short action stories are typically snippets of a key event or scene in a life extracted from fiction, a biography, or autobiography. Long action stories are biographies or biographical sketches that show a way of life.

The story (likely a "tall tale") of the first U.S. president, George Washington, as a boy chopping down a cherry tree and then not lying about it when confronted by his parents, is an action story. Stories of heroism in the face of long odds, of care for friends and family despite poverty and disease, of fidelity to a mate in the face of suggestive temptation, and of devoted service to others out of a faith commitment are other kinds of action stories. Action stories are often said to have a moral, but it is better to say that they have a point: to school those who want to learn how to swim in a particular stream of faith.

The life of Mother Teresa of Calcutta (1910–97) is an action story that has inspired many. Born in Albania, she joined the Irish Sisters of Loreto in 1928, and eventually went to India. Two decades later she was inspired to found the Missionaries of Charity to work with the poorest of the poor, especially attending their illnesses. Many joined her order, and it spread throughout the world. At the time of her death over four thousand people in over one hundred nations had joined the women's or men's orders she founded. During her life she received much recognition and numerous awards, including the Nobel Peace Prize in 1979.

After Mother Teresa died, it was revealed that she suffered from a profound religious darkness. She felt alienated from God, even rejected by God. She hoped that Christ would illumine her life. Despite tremendous difficulties with her faith, she lived faithfully.

She lived a life of exemplary service, keeping her commitment to God despite the emptiness she felt.

Mother Teresa is recognized for her heroic deeds by those of her own Roman Catholic faith tradition and by many from other traditions. She was criticized during her life for working within a social, political, and economic status quo that impoverished the people with whom she worked and not making any major attempts to reform the system that kept the poor in poverty. Nonetheless, the stories of her actions inspired many to reflect on their own basic faith and values and how the life they were leading measured up to the faith they professed.

A humanist's action story can be found in the science-fiction novel *Double Star* (1956) by Robert Heinlein. A ham actor and mimic, Lorenzo Smythe, is hired to double for politician John Joseph Bonforte at an event Bonforte cannot miss. Bonforte was leader of the Expansionist Party, a member of the general assembly of planets, and past (and future) supreme minister. He is to be the first human to be adopted into a Martian extended family. But Bonforte had been abducted by his opponents in the Humanity Party—really, the Humanity First or Humanity Only party—to ensure that he could not participate in the ceremony. He would be disgraced. War might even ensue. Smythe struggles with his own fears and his revulsion at the smell of the Martians, but he makes it through the ceremony with the help of Bonforte's friends and staff. Bonforte is then discovered, but he is so seriously injured that his aides ask Smythe to continue the impersonation through a crucial political campaign.

Smythe had to decide whether to give up his own identity for a time in order to campaign in Bonforte's place. He had his own life to live. Why should he take on this role? What did he live by? He reflected as follows:

> "The show must go on." I had always believed that and lived by it. But why must the show go on?—seeing that some shows are pretty terrible. Well, because you agreed to do it, because there is an audience out there; they have paid and each one of them is entitled to the best you can give. You

owe it to them. You owe it also to stagehands and manager and producer and other members of the company—and to those who taught you your trade and to others stretching back in history to open-air theaters and stone seats and even storytellers squatting in a market place. *Noblesse oblige.*

I decided that the notion could be generalized to any occupation. "Value for value." Building "on the square and on the level." The Hippocratic Oath. Don't let the team down. . . .

I suddenly got a glimpse of what Bonforte was driving at. If there were ethical basics that transcended time and place, then they were true for both Martians and for men. They were true on any planet around any star—and if the human race did not behave accordingly they weren't ever going to win to the stars because some better race would slap them down for double-dealing. . . .

I decided that Bonforte was my kind of man. Or at least the kind I liked to think I was. His was a *persona* I was proud to wear.

Smythe-Bonforte wins the election, and then Bonforte dies of his injuries. Smythe realizes he must give up his own life and become Bonforte. With the help of Bonforte's friends, he does so.

The epilogue reveals the truth about the story. It is set decades after the main story. Smythe as Bonforte had gone on to serve as a great-hearted major public figure. He had been in and out of office. He had, among other things, successfully fought to include nonhuman peoples in the general assembly. In the epilogue he looked back ruefully on the man he had been when he wrote the story. He had written it to get his own head straight as he gave up his life as Smythe and became Bonforte for the world.

This action story is set (as were so many classic science-fiction tales) in a fictional world similar in important aspects to our own world. One point of such fiction is to enable us to reflect on our own fundamental commitments and actions in our world. How far does our partisanship extend? To our own species? To our own ethnic group? To our nation? To our own race? Or to all peoples, human or not? Despite numerous obstacles, Smythe accepts the chance to live out the moral commitments he had as Smythe but now to act on the widest stage possible as Bonforte.

Heinlein's story makes no appeal to religion or religious support for Smythe's or Bonforte's values. It is a thoroughly secular story—but one that expands the borders of humanism. Nonetheless, even those who are not secular humanists can appreciate the point of this story. I surely do. Reading it as a young man helped me articulate my own faith better. Similarly, non-Christians may be able to learn something about themselves, what they believe in, or how they should live from Mother Teresa's story. Well-crafted action stories, both true and fictional, can show how we can and should live and act in the world—sometimes even if we do not share the faith of the community or the school that uses that particular story to teach the shape of its faith and to show its contours.

Parables

While a myth sets up a world and a saga tells you that you have come to your proper place in the world and built your temple in just the right place, a parable is *a story that upsets a world* (or one of a world's components). A parable tells you that your temple is right on the San Andreas Fault and that an earthquake might destroy it at any time. Parables are stories that destabilize other stories.

Parables are like jokes. And like jokes, they assume that the hearer has a lot of background information. The person telling the joke or narrating the parable trades on that information. The speaker then twists what the hearer knows in an unexpected way. Hearers then have to "get" the joke to laugh at it or to "get" the parable to recognize that their understanding of the world, or part of it, isn't quite as stable as they thought. Just as jokes can fall flat, so can parables. Sometimes the joke or parable is not well crafted. Sometimes the hearers just don't "get" it.

In a culture that values equal pay for equal work, a story Jesus tells, as recorded in chapter 20 of the Gospel of Matthew, functions as a parable. The story is of a vineyard owner who goes out at 6 a.m. to hire workers for the vineyard. The owner then goes

out again at 9 a.m., noon, and 3 p.m. to hire additional workers.
He tells all of them that they'll be fairly paid. When he finds some
laborers unemployed at 5 p.m., he also sends them to work in the
vineyard. At the end of the work day at 6 p.m., the owner instructs
his manager to pay them all the same. Those hired early in the day
grumble at receiving the same wage as those who worked little.
The owner notes that he paid the workers what he had promised.
It was his choice to give the last hired the same as the first hired.
The owner concludes, "May I not do what I choose with what
belongs to me? Do you object to my being generous?"

Most interpreters take the parable to be about God's generos-
ity. Or God's freedom. Or God's unfairness by human standards.
Or . . .

The problem is that no matter how one interprets this text, it
upsets our ordinary cultural expectations of equal reward for equal
work. Thus, whatever myths we have about God's justice, if they
are modeled on ordinary human accounts of justice, then they are
upset by this parable. God's justice, it says, is beyond our imagination.

In the Buddhist scripture *Milindapañha*, the monk Nagasena
explains the *anatta* doctrine to King Milinda. He, Nagasena (and
by implication, the king himself), has no soul or "I" that is the
"real" person. We ordinarily think that my name designates a real
person—me. However, Nagasena claims that a name is simply a
term of convenience; it designates nothing enduring. Nagasena
uses an analogy with a chariot to make his point. Nagasena asks
the king if a chariot is some thing other than the "combination of
pole, axle, wheels, framework, flag-staff, yoke, reins and goad?"
The king replies, "No." As the chariot is not identified with any of
the component parts, Nagasena claims, but only with their assemblage that lasts only for a time, so human persons are not identified with any of their component parts but are assemblages of
parts that last for a time. Just as the chariot has no "soul" that
binds together the parts that compose it, so a human being has no
"soul" that binds its parts together. Our names are simply convenient designators of the temporary assemblage of stuff designated
by "I."

Some Indian and Greek traditions claimed that a human being had a soul. For some Hindus, it was nothing other than the "soul" of the universe ("Atman is Brahman"). For many Greeks the soul was the form that held the body together. Nagasena used the chariot parable to upset the myths of the soul. What had been the king's (and others') stable belief about human nature was destabilized by Nagasena. His chariot analogy was a true parable.

Unlike the other genres, parables cannot be compared to one another. You may find one parable better than another, as you find one joke funnier than another. But parables are destabilizing stories. Hence, they are linked to specific stable beliefs or attitudes. So comparing them is not especially helpful.

The point of this section is to note that stories of faith are found in various genres that have different functions. Not all stories of faith are myths. Many assume that myths are found only in religion. But nonreligious secular humanists also have myths (of the ultimate origin and destiny of the world as meaningless apart from humanity), sagas (for example, of the rise of science despite religious opposition), action stories (*Double Star* is an example), and parables (especially stories that show the chaos in and the unpredictability of the way the world behaves despite the "certainties" of science). These are stories of faith, and not only stories found in religious faith traditions.

Not all faith traditions have stories in all genres. Many Buddhist traditions reject metaphysical speculation and would be wary of myths. Some people's faiths have little or no use for parables. Humanists utilize biographies to show how and why they became humanists, but sagas—stories of a people—do not seem to fit a humanist's faith very well, unless one considers scientists a people.

Stories flesh out the answer to those crucial questions of faith: What do I live for ultimately? What is or are the irreducible center(s) of value and source(s) of meaning in my life? Most important, narratives show us how to live a faith, that is, what a faithful person worships and what a faithful person may need to give up, to sacrifice.

SYMBOLS OF FAITH

To explore the significance of symbols, we can begin with a story.

Once upon a time, a Roman Catholic graduate student was assisting a professor in a course on church history in a Protestant seminary. The course was a graduation requirement for students studying for the Protestant ministry. After class one day, a "student pastor" (a ministry student who already preached in a church) from the hills of North Carolina approached her.

"Can I ask you a question about Catholics?" he inquired.

"Sure," she responded.

"Well, I've always wondered about this question—I don't mean to be offensive, but . . . ," he said shyly. Then he blurted out his real question, "Why do Catholics worship statues?"

"How interesting. What makes you think Catholics worship statues?"

"Well, I've seen 'em praying to the statues and my own pastor told me that's what they were doing, too."

The teaching assistant chuckled. The student pastor saw Catholics as idolaters, profoundly unfaithful to God, worshiping statues as if they were gods. The teaching assistant then explained Catholic practice as a way of clarifying his misconceptions.

She told him that Catholics do not "worship statues." Rather, statues are *images* of Christ and the saints. They are not gods. Mary is not a goddess. The statues are symbols that focus the attention of the one who prays on what is symbolized. God and the saints are the object of their prayers, not the statues. To take the statues as gods is overly literal. Catholics do not worship statues. They pray to or venerate what the statues symbolize.

The student recognized the symbol but got its significance wrong. To correct the student, the graduate assistant had to explain how the Catholic story places the saints and their statues. She needed to school him in the stories of the Catholic faith. He got the significance wrong not because he didn't recognize the symbols—he did—but because he did not understand how to place those symbols properly in the context of practicing a Catholic faith.

Using Images

Of course, one can reject the use of images. An iconoclastic attitude at least suspects and often rejects the use of images. Muslims reject using pictorial images of God and Mohammed the messenger. Many Muslims reject images of humans. Jews reject making images of God. Some Protestants reject the use of images like statues or stained glass windows. Yet each of these faiths uses bell towers or minarets that point to the heavens, to God. While not pictorial images, such architecture nonetheless shapes the imagination of participants.

Nonetheless, many members of faith communities use images as symbols. Catholics may pray to God as they meditate on a crucifix. This symbol represents the execution of Jesus, the Son of God, and its significance in saving humanity from sin. The crucifix helps their focus and concentration as they pray, but they do not worship the crucifix. Far from it! They worship the god whose powerful love for humanity is symbolized in the crucifix. Analogously, many Hindus receive *darsan* as they gaze on the images of their god. Once the images have been constructed and dedicated, they make the god present. Devotees do not merely look at the god. Rather, the god gives them their sight.

Devotees do not so much pray *to* images as pray *with* images and *through* images. The statues, crucifixes, and the bread and wine devotees see are not the objects of their veneration but are symbols *for* the object(s) of prayer and veneration. Catholics traditionally believe that Jesus Christ is really present in the bread and wine at communion; hence, they treat the elements with great reverence and devotion. Hindus traditionally believe that the image (which may or may not picture a god) in the context of worship in the temple is the god really present. Hence, they ritually treat the statue with great devotion as the real presence of the god.

Christians may pray to the saints to intercede with God for them, but it is God who is the focus of their prayers, and the saints are taken as people who pray along in particular circumstances. Hindus may seek *darsan* from saints and imitate aspects of their lives or their religious practices. Christians may also meditate on the inspiring lives of saints. They can also ask the saints (whom Catholics believe live on in the afterlife with God) to help them or to ask God to help them. Stories of saints are models for life, action stories, as discussed above. Prayer to the saints or seeking *darsan* from a saint or holy person can be a way of focusing one's own life on the model that the saint provides.

Iconoclasts worry (or believe) that those who use images are idolaters, that is, people who worship statues or images rather than what the images make present. Admittedly, venerating images can become idolatrous. Those of us who use images need to take iconoclasm as a serious and sometimes salient warning. But if we use images well, then the iconoclastic argument is not a threat, but rather a parabolic reminder that we must not believe that symbols and images can exhaust or are the realities they represent.

The Status of Symbols

Sometimes one hears the phrase "only a symbol" or "merely a symbol." A symbol of faith is *never* "merely" or "only." Desecrating the Holy Qur'an by throwing it on the ground and stomping on it evokes cries of pain from Muslims. For non-Muslims the Qur'an may be "only a book" that "symbolizes" the Islamic tradition, but a sacred book is *never* "only a book." The Qur'an contains or transmits the eternal truth. The bread and wine that is blessed and consumed when Christians celebrate the Lord's supper, communion, the mass, or the eucharist (various Christian denominations use different terminology) is often said to "symbolize" the body and blood of Christ. But whether one is a traditional Roman Catholic who believes in the "Real Presence" of Christ in the sacrament of the eucharist (Christ is actually there) or a Baptist who takes the Lord's supper as an ordinance that commemorates the Lord, the symbols of bread and wine in that ritual context are never "merely." Their meanings are powerful and deeply expressive of the faith of those who engage in the rituals.

A symbol can be simply defined as *a visible or audible image that focuses one's faith*. The term *symbol,* of course, has many meanings beyond designating items of faith. But each of those meanings is determined by how people use the symbols and the context in which they use them. Mathematical symbols do not stand for an object of faith; they are conventional signs that we acknowledge have a particular significance in equations. Corporate symbols are designed to attract attention to a corporation or its products; they do not focus faith, but they keep a corporation in the mind of those who see the sign, such as the image of the apple on the lids of Macintosh notebook computers.

These symbols in mathematics, advertising, and other places are what theologian Paul Tillich called "signs." People intentionally invent signs to stand for things. These signs then become ordinary conventions that people come to accept. Consider the red octagon of the stop sign on a street. It is arbitrary—a stop sign could easily have been another shape or color. These signs do not represent or present something else. They are what they are. They are "opaque" to further significance.

Some representational signs, like the symbols of faith and unlike stop signs, may be conventional images designed to call to mind something beyond them. They may be relatively arbitrary (as is the stylized swoosh symbol used by Nike sporting goods, or the chimes of the NBC Television Network) or a rather obvious fit (as is the apple symbol for Apple computers or the heart with a chunk missing in the "I love NY more than ever" logo by Milton Glaser, an update to the original 1970s "I love NY" logo following 9/11). Like faith symbols, these representational signs evoke responses to something beyond the signs. But these signs are not our concern here.

The symbols of faith are usually fitting, multivalent, and relatively transparent. The cross is a fitting symbol for Christians because it is rooted in the way Jesus was executed. It is multivalent in that it has a number of meanings for Christians. It is relatively transparent in that it is not the literal wood of the cross that is important but what happened in the execution of Jesus. The wood and the shape are images. The image of Buddha sitting in the lotus position of meditation is fitting for Buddhists. It is multivalent in that it can symbolize the Buddha's patience, serenity, peace, compassion, and so on. It is relatively transparent because the use of the symbol by Buddhists does not assume that it pictures Gautama Siddhartha or any particular image but shows what the Buddha-essence is or what it is that Buddhists seek.

Symbols are not only visual. They may be spoken and heard as well. The Qur'an transparently reveals God's will for humanity, even though just what that will is may divide Muslims. The reciting of the Qur'an, the singing of a hymn, the reading aloud and hearing of a passage from the Bible, and the preaching of a religious leader may also be symbols of faith.

If one does not understand how the symbols function for those who live in a particular myth and engage in appropriate practices, one cannot "get" what they mean. The story of the seminarian told earlier exemplifies this. He could not see how statues appeared to Catholics because he was ignorant of the Catholic myth and the way Catholics pray. He had not been schooled in the right way to view statues in the Catholic tradition. Thus, he took the statues as the objects of veneration, not transparent symbols of what is venerated.

People often find the point of symbols in the context of ritual. The practice of stopping baseball games for the crowd to sing "America, the Beautiful," begun in some major league baseball parks after the attack on the World Trade Center on 9/11, is a ritual that reinforces the meaning of the American flag as a symbol. The placing of the Bible on a lectern during a worship service reinforces for the congregation the symbolic significance of the Bible. To understand a symbol properly, one often has to understand how it is used in practice.

This is not to say that some people do not treat images as gods. They do. But for *most* religious traditions, the images are not a god but symbolize a god, make real the presence of a god, a god's will, or another person who has been devoted to doing the will of a god (a saint). The images work for the people venerating the symbol or praying through the image to what is imaged. One understands the *use* of images in a tradition by the *place* they have in the tradition's myth.

Ranking Symbols

In faith traditions symbols can be ranked or ordered. The statues of the saints, for example, are symbols that are meaningful and valuable to the Catholic tradition because of the saints' devotion to God. Their value is not independent of faith in God. These symbols are valuable to a Catholic because the saints are exemplars of faith in God. Their stories display excellent ways of being a Christian. The saints may be sources of value and centers of meaning in people's lives, but they are not *irreducible*. Their value and meaning derive from God. They cannot be placed above God or alongside God. They are ordered to faith in God in the Catholic faith tradition.

Obviously, to any who know traditional Catholics, some saints occupy a large place in the lives of their devotees. But saints are servants of God. To place a saint above or alongside God would be idolatry in Catholicism. It would be a disorder. It would get the Catholic myth wrong and thus get the proper placing or ranking of the symbol wrong.

The ordering of symbols can be a key to understanding conflicts in faith. Take a national flag, for example. For a henotheist, the flag can symbolize one's god: the nation. Desecrating the flag is a sacrilege. The flag is respected in the times and ways it is flown, the way it is folded when stored, and the use one makes of it in general. For those whose irreducible source of meaning and center of value are their country, the flag symbolizes their god.

Yet a patriot who is a monotheistic Christian or Muslim in the military service of the country, for example, might treat the flag with the same care and respect as does a nationalistic henotheist serving in the military. But whereas the henotheist recognizes no god beyond the nation, the monotheist is committed to a god beyond the nation that is the source of meaning and center of value. The difference is between "one nation under God" and "one nation that is our god." The nation's value is secondary or derivative for the monotheist, but ultimate and irreducible for the henotheistic nationalist. The reasons each respects the flag and the way that symbol fits in the practice of each one's faith differ. The respect for the flag is fundamentally different because the ways the flag fits as a symbol in the Muslim or Christian myths and in the myth of Manifest Destiny or American exceptionalism differ greatly.

What happens when one's faith conflicts with one's duty to one's country? Note that for the henotheistic patriot, such a conflict is impossible. But patriotic Lutherans, for example, who love their country can develop such conflicts. For example, if they are ordered by a superior military officer to engage in an act that contradicts the moral code of their faith, there is a conflict between their patriotism and their faith. Is the Christian cross or the American flag the symbol of the faith one actually practices? Which is the story, the myth, that shapes one's world? Conflicts bring up such questions and force us to rank the symbols in our lives.

The important point here is to understand how the symbol fits into one's life. If one's irreducible source of value is the God of Christianity, then one's faith may be symbolized in the cross. If one obeys an immoral order from a military superior rather than resists it, then one is treating the nation as superior to the cross. Then the flag symbolizes one's god. The place that the symbol has in one's life reveals the contours of one's true faith. Does one pay the price for disobedience to orders on the basis of the moral values of a good Lutheran? Or does one silence one's objections and carry out the order?

When our values conflict, what we do and what we sacrifice reveals our faith—and our true god. Our choices show which symbol gives value and meaning to other symbols, which symbol presents us with the source of meaning, and which symbols present us with something that is meaningful but not the source of meaning. Our choices show which image symbolizes our true faith. For one who claims to be a Christian, does the cross or the flag symbolize the god in whom one has faith? Which is primary and irreducible, which secondary and derivative in significance from the irreducible center of meaning and source of value?

One's pattern of actions may be quite similar to another's even if their faiths differ. Earlier we sketched the lives of the real Dag

Hammarskjöld and the fictional Joseph Bonforte. Both gave their lives to working for peace among peoples—as shown in the epilogue to *Double Star* for Bonforte and the documented life of Hammarskjöld. But whereas Bonforte's faith was rooted in inclusive humanistic principles, Hammarskjöld's faith was rooted in Christianity, as shown in his posthumously published journal, *Markings*. That publication surprised many people who had not known he was Christian. The point is that we may not know which faith someone is practicing: two or more people may share many values and live very similar lives, but each way of living may be rooted in a different faith. To recognize the difference, we'd have to know which creeds, which stories, which symbols express their commitments to the *irreducible* center of value and source of meaning for each of them.

The symbols discussed in this section receive their focal meaning in the practices of a faith, especially the practice of telling stories. Many of these practices are learned in the context of a faith community that teaches or shows us how to live in and live out a faith.

PRACTICES OF FAITH

Professing creeds, telling stories, and using symbols are, of course, practices in which people of faith engage. So far we have focused on the *content* of the practices. Here we focus on particular kinds of practice associated with faith.

Like any other relationship, faith involves not only believing in the other to whom one is related, but doing for and receiving from the other. Chapter 2 claimed we had to learn how to have faith. Here we explore the practices we learn how to perform as we develop the relationship that is faith.

Like playing the violin, riding a bicycle, working complex mathematical problems, or programming a computer, having faith is not a yes or no thing. People can be virtuoso violinists or learning to fiddle. Both an Olympic medalist and I can swim, but there is a huge difference in skill levels. As in these varied practices, the practitioner of a faith may be a novice or an expert.

The relationship that is faith is a set of practices composed of patterns of acting, believing, and attitudes (including feelings). The elements of such practices are so woven together that they can be distinguished analytically but not separated practically. As noted in Chapter 2, it is possible to distinguish, but not separate, the subjects and objects in the faith relationship. Similarly, the patterns involved in practicing a faith can be distinguished analytically but not separated in practice. Within a faith tradition, a set of central and distinctive beliefs fits within a web of actions and attitudes. Thus, to understand a given belief, action, or attitude, one has to understand how it fits in the web. Abstracting any particular element from the web for purposes of analysis surely is legitimate. But ignoring those connections can be an instance of the rationalist misunderstanding of faith discussed in Chapter 1.

Attitudes about oneself, one's family, one's community, one's society, and one's world are inscribed in the creeds, stories, symbols, and practices of a faith. Learning them properly teaches one how to live the faith of that tradition. Part of understanding faith is to understand the overarching attitudes toward the whole world and each of the human spheres (personal, interpersonal, familial, communal, tribal, organizational, national, natural) within it. The world may be nothing but *maya* (illusion), as Hindu scriptures suggest (see, for example, *Bhagavad Gita* 18:61). With such an attitude various meditation practices can be prescribed for penetrating the veil of illusion or for understanding the manifoldness of everything or for seeing the Dancer in the dancing. Or the world may be a garden created by a god for us to live in. Then seeing our tending it as the proper attitude for getting on with our life would fit. Attitudes make a difference about how one lives; meditating is not gardening, even though one can meditate while gardening.

Often philosophers overlook the importance of such attitudes and collapse them into merely cognitive beliefs. But that will not do. For instance, some Christians have said that one cannot be a Christian until one realizes one is a sinner. One has to *take oneself to be* a sinner. This is not merely a belief one holds true. It involves an important attitude to all of one's life. It is not a nominal belief, whose meaning can be captured in a bare proposition, but a conviction that shapes one's life; to realize the significance of this conviction requires learning how to be a sinner. For if one does not realize that one is a sinner, then one cannot realize that one has been redeemed from sin.

Attitudes are important. Buddhists, for example, often seek Enlightenment as the goal of life. That is not only a belief about what the goal of life is or ought to be, but it involves a very complex attitude that is not grasping desire for Enlightenment, not indifference to Enlightenment, not the construal of Enlightenment as an individual achievement for which one can take credit, not as a gratuitous gift that one does not even accept. The full range of human emotions and attitudes, from fear to trust, hope to despair, empowerment to powerlessness, joy to sorrow, wondering awe to disdain, are rooted in one's faith.

For analytical purposes most scholars divide the answers to such questions about how to practice a faith into the areas of morality and ritual. Moral prescriptions and proscriptions focus on actions that shape our relationships with ourselves, our family, our friends, our community, our nation, and the environment. Ritual prescriptions and proscriptions shape our relationship with our god. They teach us how to worship, show us the significance of symbols, and unite us as a community of faith. In practice, of course, ritual practice and moral practice cannot be separated so easily, but distinguishing them for analytical purposes helps us explore the practices of faith.

Ritual Practices and Faith

Ritual practices shape one's faith. When the priest at a Roman Catholic mass engages in gestures highlighting the consecration of the bread and wine, those gestures evoke an attitude of reverence. When people kneel and pray for forgiveness, they make real the belief that they are sinners. When the American flag is brought into an arena or stadium before a sporting event and the national anthem is sung, the ritual practice unites the people who participate and shapes their attitudes toward the country and the flag that symbolizes it. Ritual practices shape one's attitudes, including attitudes about oneself.

Changes in ritual practice can change one's formulations of one's beliefs. For example, the changes in the ritual practices of the Roman Catholics significantly affected their beliefs. Celebrating the mass in Latin (the standard practice before the Second Vatican Council in the 1960s) with the priest "leading the people" (or as most Catholics seemed to have perceived it, with his back to the congregation), highlighted the mystery. The mass reenacted the sacrifice of Christ when he accepted crucifixion on Calvary. When the eucharist is celebrated in the people's language with the presider facing the congregation, the mass highlights the last supper that Jesus shared with his disciples the night before he was executed. Both Latin and vernacular rituals incorporate references to Holy Thursday and Good Friday.

Yet these changes in ritual affected the way Catholics understood the sacramental symbol of the bread and wine. Some bemoaned the loss of the mystery of the symbol. Others delighted in the gain of the sense of communion in the symbol. With the ritual change the emphasis changed significantly enough to affect Catholics' beliefs and attitudes.

Specific beliefs can function as presumptions or frameworks for ritual practices. For example, Roman Catholics are taught to believe in the real presence of Christ in the bread and wine of the eucharist. Such a belief undergirds the devout Catholic's attitudes about the eucharist and the way they are to regard the consecrated bread and wine. Yet Catholics learn how to believe in the real presence of Christ as much from what they do in the ritual of the mass as from formal instruction. The real significance of the symbol is learned by being schooled in a devotional practice, even if beliefs about the symbol are taken as a foundation for the practice.

We are typically schooled in the practice of faith. We learn what it means as we learn how to proclaim a creed, narrate a myth, use a symbol, or explore a belief. Schools of faith teach which actions and practices to perform and which to avoid. They offer answers to practical questions. What must I do to be a good or true Buddhist or Baptist? How can I live as a left-handed Tantrist or a Sivite? What should a secular humanist like me do now? How can a good American show respect for the country? Of course, not one of these questions is meaningful to us if we know little or nothing about such traditions. But if a faith is a "living option," that is, if we know something about a faith tradition and that faith appeals to us, then those questions may be significant, and learning the answers—even if we do not take up a particular faith tradition in which the answer is at home—may help us shape the contours of our lives.

Members of a tradition ordinarily participate in its ritual practices. A tradition may carry and be carried by life-cycle rituals, practices undertaken at the key transitions in life from birth to death. Calendar rituals may be performed on a weekly, monthly, or annual basis as ways of marking and dedicating the life of the individual and community. There may be crisis rituals designed to dedicate oneself or to implore the mercy of the powers that be in times of unexpected crisis from illness to famine to war.

Even the most austere faith traditions incorporate rituals. A henotheistic patriot devoutly salutes the flag. A secular humanist may marry ceremoniously. Science has its protocols, such as the double-blind testing in clinical trials of experimental drugs. If one is a scientific rationalist, such protocols can function as the rituals of one's faith. Some traditions are "austere" just because their rituals are minimal or latent rather than richly executed and patent. Learning how to participate in such rituals is part of learning a faith.

Learning how to participate in others' rituals is also a part of the practice of faith. It may be only good manners, but many find good manners important. Buddhists and humanists may respect and enjoy a bar mitzvah, but it is not a rite in their life-cycle. And traditionally religious people who work in science follow protocols but do not take them as the rituals of a "scientistic" faith. Whether one should participate in others' rituals and how to do so can be a matter of serious disagreement.

Moral Practices and Faith

To live out a faith one may perform specific acts and avoid other acts. One may have to avoid specific people and places. One must work to develop in oneself and others specific character traits.

No good Southern Baptist could frequent a house of prostitution. No good Theravadin monk could seek employment as a butcher. And according to the great twelfth-century thinker Moses Maimonides, Judaism has two hundred forty-eight positive commandments and three hundred sixty-five negative ones. These rules are not so much guides for people who already believe as they are principles that teach people how to live. And living includes believing. These acts are part of learning how to have faith in one's god.

The connection of actions with faith is important. For when we act, we act for reasons or purposes. Sometimes these are implicit, sometimes explicit. There may be no visible difference when a nationalistic henotheist and a Jewish monotheist salute a flag. Both may act patriotically. What makes their actions different is the purpose each has in performing them. Is it worship, however implicit? Or is it respect? What two people are doing may look the same but be different if their purposes are different or if they differ in faith.

When seeking to understand a faith, one cannot neglect its moral component. When examining a particular faith, one cannot reduce it to moral acts or practices, as Chapter 1 argued. But neither can one neglect the practices that express that faith in action. Even if one does not accept all the claims made in *The Protestant Ethic and the Spirit of Capitalism*, Max Weber showed a century ago that there are links between worldly success and belief and practice in the Calvinist strand of the Christian tradition. Even if one does not accept all the critiques feminists make of religious traditions, they have shown that many traditions have been and are not immune to sexism and have at times encouraged the subjugation of women. Recognizing and understanding such links between moral practices and beliefs are essential for understanding.

CONCLUSION

To understand a faith, then, one understands the set of practices that shapes the relationship one has with one's god and with everything else. The relationship includes interlinked patterns of actions, beliefs, and attitudes. These practices show the force of the creeds, the practical significance of the stories, and the meanings of the symbols used to express the faith. To understand a faith, then, is not merely to know what people believe, but to know how people live in and live out their faith. It is our lives that show what we worship and what we need to sacrifice in order to worship well. Our lives show what our faith is and means, what our irreducible source(s) of value and center(s) of meaning are.

But simply to lay out these verbal and vital expressions of faith is only part of the task. We also need to evaluate these faiths. For many of us both secular humanism and a particular religious tradition may be "live options." For many of us our lives are formed so that they might fit many faiths. We are in a position analogous to narrators of Hammarskjöld's life and Bonforte's life in politics. Our story—at least as told so far—might be a story that fits more than one tradition. In order to understand which faith is and should be ours, we must seek to take another step in theology: justifying faith.

5

Justifying Faith

At the time of the Reformation, Catholics and Protestants fought over whether a person was justified by faith. Protestants mostly said "yes, by faith alone." Catholics said, "yes, but good works are necessary, too." That debate still frames how believers connect faith with justification. However, this chapter is not involved in those polemics. To paraphrase the ancient Greek philosopher Socrates, who said an unexamined life is not worth living, I say an unexamined faith is not worth believing. The question we ask here is not whether our faith justifies us, but whether we are justified in holding our faith in light of the diversity of faiths in our culture. This chapter lays out criteria that we can employ to answer this question.

ASSESSING FAITH

To understand the practical significance of a relationship, one must "come to judgment" about it. This is the process of justifying the relationships. Is the way Sandy and Jamie relate good for them? Might their relationship be a model for my beloved and me? Should I raise my kids the way my parents raised me? Something analogous can be said about understanding the relationship we call faith. We have to come to judgment about our own faith and perhaps the faiths of others.

There are some common-sense questions we can ask to assess human relationships. Do the partners support each other? Is their relationship balanced? Are they happy? Do the kids thrive? Most of the time we don't examine or assess the relationships of other people. But sometimes—especially when relationships are strained—we cannot avoid such evaluation.

When it comes to faith, we also tend to avoid examination and assessment. We sometimes take faith as beyond question. However, like our other relationships, our faith relationships may be very personal, but, as we have noted repeatedly in earlier chapters, they are not private. We need to ask questions and find criteria that can serve to help us assess whether our faith relationships are justified, just as common-sense criteria serve to help us assess personal relationships.

For some, the answer to the key question is obvious: If I have faith in the only living and true god, then I *should* have faith in that god. That faith will straighten me out and set me on a true path. It will justify me. On the other hand, if my god is not truly god, then I should not have faith in that god. Faith in that god is liable to make me crooked or misshapen and inclined to navigate a false path. So, the first question should not be whether my faith justifies me, but whether I am justified in holding my faith. More generally: How do we understand which of the many divinities in which humans have faith is (are) worthy of *our* faith—our worship and our sacrifice?

Unwarranted Assumptions?

We cannot just assume that our god is the only faith-worthy god. We live in a multi-faith society. We recognize people as good and smart who do not share our faith. We cannot merely *assume* that we've got it right. Reflection and assessment help us better understand the assumptions we have made. Such work also should help us to articulate our faith more clearly.

We cannot simply judge faiths by the standards implicit in our own myth or articulated in our stories, creeds, and symbols. The diversity of myths and faiths does not show that ours are wrong, but it does show that there are other standards that other good and intelligent people accept. It is disrespectful to assume that they are wrong. As we cannot assume our faiths to be unquestion-able, so we cannot assume that our faith prescribes the right stan-dards.

And even if our faith is in God, the question of how to live out our faith—not only whether to be Jews, Christians, or Muslims, but also what sort of Jews, Christians, or Muslims to be—requires an answer. Are we warriors or pacifists in our faith? Should we work with those of other faiths or go it alone in responding to human needs? Should we be involved in politics or not? Hence, the "obvious" answer noted above may be formally correct, but it is materially inadequate. It does not help us understand which god, if any, among so many gods that humans revere ought to be our god or gods or what sort of relationship we should have with that god or gods.

It is ordinarily appropriate to assume that our faith is right and true. And it is that *assumption* that diversity in faith calls into question. Assessing faith is the practice of resolving the issues raised by religious diversity. What we are *not* calling into ques-tion is one's faith in one's god. What we cannot avoid calling into question is the *assumption* that one's faith is a right relationship with the truly divine. To question my assumptions is not to doubt my faith. It is to examine and understand my faith in the context of diversity.

One does not and cannot abandon one's faith when one is en-gaging in the work of justifying faith. Persons of faith cannot avoid assessing the faith they express because various experiences chal-lenge that faith. Whatever position persons of faith take on a seri-ously debated and morally charged political issue (for example, should gay marriages or unions be legalized, should our country invade another, should a government prohibit suicide—all are examples of difficult issues as I write), we will have to understand and assess how best to express our faith in response to such chal-lenges. And it is possible that we will discover what our faith really is in response to such challenges. It is even possible that our faith may change in response to such challenges, sometimes radically.

Those challenges are not merely external. In a diverse society we are pushed and pulled in many directions. Our diverse society gives us varied political, moral, aesthetic, and educational values, some of which we accept and others we ignore or reject. We seek a good life, and so we value financial success and pleasurable activities. Some of us also have explicitly religious values. Which of these values are primary? That is, which of these can we see as our irreducible source(s) of meaning and center(s) of value? These are the values that are internal to us. How can we order those values? How can we understand what our real faith is? How can we discover the god that is the *source* of the value of the many items we value? How ought we live out our relationship to the source of the values we hold and the meaning we find in our lives? The answers to these questions cannot be taken for granted. We have to reflect on them.

The reality of such challenges means that we cannot avoid having the courage of faith. The courageous person realizes that faith is always a risk—I have bet my life and that bet might be wrong, even though I believe it is right. I bet my life. That is why assessing faith is a necessary task in the face of challenges to faith.

The chapter title indicates that, whatever faith we are assessing, we cannot do so from some "faith-neutral" perspective. We bring our faith with us to the table when we seek to understand and assess faith—our own or that of others. As we understand others' faiths sympathetically, we can see how their insights can complement (or challenge) our own. Even if we can avoid assessing others' faith, we cannot avoid assessing our own—unless, of course, we disagree with Socrates and think that the unexamined life *is* worth living.

Constructing Faith

Some would say that there's a shortcut to this process. Just forget all this faith stuff and live without faith. But the story we mentioned in the Introduction reminds us that, aware of it or not, we live in faith as fish live in water. And too often, like the young fish in the story, we ask, "What the hell is faith?" By this time, I hope you have formed at least a tentative answer to that question. We need to learn how to understand and assess what we take for granted, including our faith.

Undoubtedly, some will find David Wallace Foster, whose version of the fish story I quoted in the Introduction (and me, too) mistaken. They may offer a sophisticated version of this shortcut by claiming that the gods to which our faith relates us are projections, so no assessment is needed. If all the gods are bogus, then the relationships of faith with them don't really matter. We should just live without them.

In Chapter 1 we noted that Freud claimed that religious beliefs used to express faith were illusions; we believe them because we wish them to be true. If this view were accurate, then no faith could be justified. If the gods are projections, we should abandon faith in god and in gods for the illusion faith is.

The easy answer to this challenge is implied in our earlier work and in the comment on Wallace's parable. No one, even the scientific secular humanist, lives without some sort of faith. If all faith is illusory, then the question is which illusions should be ours. The attempt to live without faith is at least a confusion and, at worst, a delusion. We can't avoid living in faith; we can't just ignore faith any more than we can simply assume it without question. The question is *not* whether to have faith, but *which* faith can I be justified in holding? While I think this a sufficient response to the challenge, some more sophisticated skeptics might find it inadequate. Those who still find projection theories persuasive can find a further argument against this challenge in the Appendix.

Assessing Faith

Faith is a relationship. We express it in creeds, stories, symbols, and practices. I propose that we develop appropriate criteria to assess or appraise the expressions of faith. I suggest that we can base these criteria on the ways we use the term *true* in our everyday language. Those expressions that we can find true, then, would indicate whether the faith they express is justified.

We assess many claims by common sense. We assess others by the skilled use of criteria developed by experts in a practice. Each practice—from investigating crimes to evaluating property, to solving linear equations, to psychological and physical diagnosis of clients and patients—has developed distinct criteria. What are the conditions and criteria for assessing faith?

Conditions

Assessing claims is a practice undertaken in specific conditions. First, there can be no appeal to a practice-independent "cause" of our claims to be the "warrant" for our claims. In Chapter 1 we developed the notion of final fact parity, showing that "final facts" cannot be further explained. Different faiths posit different final facts. Some have suggested that the world in which we live is "intellectually ambiguous" because a number of "final facts" fit the world we know pretty well. A number of faiths and the myths and creeds that express them also fit the world as we know it fairly well. As we have no access to a world independent of our understanding of it, so we have no "myth-independent" or "faith-independent" way to talk of the world. We cannot get into a position to warrant our claims that our beliefs are true (and, perhaps, others' beliefs are false) on the basis of "the world" in itself.

Second, people have faiths that were formed in the context of different faith traditions. A certain Baptist may be a very good Baptist. A particular Buddhist may be a very good Buddhist. Yet each has faith in a different source of meaning and center of value. So, if we are attempting to answer a question such as "What sort of faith does a good Buddhist have," a reliable Buddhist can help us answer it. But if we want to answer "Why not be a Buddhist?" or "Why stay a Catholic?" a reliable Buddhist or Catholic may not be very helpful. Participants in varied practices may properly and reliably develop very diverse expressions of faith. The *situation* of diversity, including final fact parity, means that having a reliably formed faith is not a sufficient answer to the question of how we can assess faiths.

Third, such diversity in the practices of faith generates a *problem* of pluralism: how are some well-formed beliefs acceptable as true when other well-formed beliefs contradict them? Since it is not possible to appeal to the-world-independent-of-our-practice-formed-beliefs and it is insufficient to appeal to beliefs-formed-reliably-in-practices as useful criteria to show whether those beliefs are justified, we must turn to a different kind of practice if we are to assess the expressions of faith.

A scientific materialist might say that science should judge. But that begs the question. It assumes the faith of scientific materialism is not also in need of justification. That assumption cannot be sustained. After all, even if all our concepts are human constructs, including our concepts of the divine, is it that religious people are "seeing" something that is *not* there or that materialists are "missing" something that *is* there? Science cannot be the final criterion.

Hence, we must work on assessing or appraising expressions of faith.

Appraisals

Many practices include a practice of appraising. The content of appraisals are truth-claims. Realtors appraise real estate, editors appraise writing, reviewers appraise arguments, consumers appraise merchandise, juries appraise guilt, judges in athletic competitions appraise performances. Each of these appraisals results in practical truth-claims. "This house is worth $247,000." "This manuscript will never be a book we can sell." "This essayist has demonstrated her point convincingly." "This shirt is not worth $22.95." "He is guilty of involuntary manslaughter, not of murder." "Her floor exercise is worth 9.7 points." These claims may be formed by people well-trained in appraisals (and thus their appraisals should be reliably formed unless other factors interfere), but that alone does not make those appraisals acceptable. All of our explicit truth-claims, from simple to complex, can be construed as the linguistic expression of practical appraisals, from "this house is worthless," to "this argument is valid," to "God's in heaven and all's well in God's world."

Sometimes we think such appraisals are wrong. One can challenge appraisals by employing other real-estate appraisers, submitting one's manuscript to another publisher, highlighting points in an essay a reviewer may have discounted, discussing the prices of comparable shirts, appealing the verdict to a higher court, or booing the gymnastics judge. Indeed, appraisals often require more than one expert (juries composed of twelve peers, panels of gymnastics judges, multiple appraisals of the cost of repairing damaged automobiles) to be construed as valid.

The condition of diversity in faith is the fundamental condition that makes assessing expressions of faith an appropriate task. Given that other people of good mind and heart differ with us in faith, the need to question the assumption that our faith is an unquestionable relationship seems obvious. If we all agreed on what the irreducible source of meaning and center of value is or should be for all of us, and if we all agreed on how to relate to that god or gods, then the issue would not arise. But it does arise.

I find five criteria useful for appraising the expressions of faith. Applying these criteria is the practice of appraisal or assessment. Here I lay out these criteria for your consideration and give you some examples. The actual work of appraisal cannot be done by a book, since making an appraisal or assessment is an act. Texts may record the acts, but texts are not acts. Finally, you have to do the appraising for yourself. No text can do it for you, no matter how helpful it might be in showing you how to do it.

APPRAISING FAITH

The project of appraising or assessing generally requires multiple standards. Real-estate appraisers, for example, use multiple measures. They look at the recent sale prices of comparable properties. They evaluate other properties on the market. They look at pricing trends. They extrapolate market value from fair rental pricing. Appraising is neither purely objective nor purely subjective. It is a judgment call.

To appraise a faith, we appraise its expressions in creeds, stories, symbols, and practices. Appraising expressions of faith also requires multiple rules by which to measure these expressions. Expressions of a complex relationship like faith are not simply factual claims. Faith is a relationship with many facets. Appraising faith requires analyzing those expressions from multiple angles.

Revealing the Hidden

A claim expressed in a story or a creed can be appraised as true if it shows the world in which we live, or a part of it, in a revealing way. A detective may lay out a case against an alleged criminal for me. I had no idea that the perpetrator (my friend!) was in any way implicated. After hearing the detective out, I might say, "Oh, my God! It's true! Jean did it, and I never suspected it."

Philosopher Martin Heidegger (1889–1976) captured this notion of truth as revealing the hidden. He reflected on the ancient Greek word for truth, *aletheia*. The letter *alpha* that begins the word is an "alpha privative," meaning that it functions the way *un* does in English. To tell the truth or to show the truth is to *un-cover* what has been hidden.

Stories sometimes reveal something we had not seen before. Sometimes we do not like revealing stories, but we can still appreciate them. By this measure, stories that evoke responses like, "Oh, my God! It's true!" or "I never saw it that way before" appraise rather well.

Parables—stories that upset our world or part of it—are designed to be revelatory. If they do not expose the cracks in the foundations of our world or the oversights in our concepts, then they fail to do what they should do. Nagasena's chariot parable worked with King Milinda to undermine his belief in a soul. Indeed, even if I do believe I have a soul, this parable uncovers the fact that we have to think long and hard about just what a soul is. And if I think that a soul is whatever provides one with a personal identity, then what about the argument implicit in Heinlein's *Double Star*? Did Smythe really become Bonforte? What was his identity? Who was he, really? Did he have one soul or two?

The point is that good parables make us rethink our assumptions. They may uncover something true that we had ignored.

Any expression of faith may show us previously unnoticed connections among the events and people of the world in which we live. A story may show us that an assumption we have made needs rethinking. Such expressions can be evaluated as true by this standard of "uncovering the hidden."

Of course, this criterion cannot stand alone. That would unhappily equate the shocking, the surprising, or the revealing with the true. There's more to truth than just unveiling. Moreover, sometimes shocking stories may be told in order to deceive the hearer, or shocking gestures—like those of a magician—may be performed to distract a viewer from what is there. Dazzlingly blinding expressions can be manipulative. People use them to dupe us, and they can evoke invalid insights. For instance, some Christians have told the story of the passion and death of Jesus with the purpose of evoking the "insight" that the Jews are or were "god-killers." However, if the purpose of narrating Jesus' passion and death is to express faith in Jesus, then an anti-Jewish telling of the story violates the true purpose of the story. It becomes a story to evoke hatred, not faith or love of Jesus, the Jewish man from Nazareth whom Christians see as God incarnate. Criteria beyond "revealing the hidden" are needed.

To assess an expression of faith one must note what that expression is supposed to do. Sometimes the purpose—of a myth or a creed—is to set up a world or map a world, not to upset a world. In those cases the present criterion of revealing the hidden might be rather less important than other criteria as we assess a myth or creed.

Assessing an expression of faith as truly revealing what has been hidden may have to be done over and over. Some expressions become so hackneyed that they no longer "uncover" something previously overlooked. Some symbols also become hackneyed. Some images can no longer be used or used rightly—if some Catholics did indeed pray to a statue, that statue, in becoming "opaque" to God for them, would fail to be revelatory. Just because an expression is revealing at some times and in some places does not mean that it will be revealing at all times and in all places. A revealing claim or performance rings true; an obscuring performance or claim is boring or hollow and thus fails to ring true.

We need ways to assess whether an expression is authentically revealing or whether it has been manipulated into seeing what is not there. Use of the next criterion is thus helpful.

Cohering

If the first criterion focuses on the *effectiveness* of an expression of faith to reveal, the second focuses on the *content* of what it reveals. An expression that fits well with other facts we recognize can be appraised as true. If a creed, saga, or other expression does not fit what we know independently of it, then this counts against its being true. While the first standard (revealing the hidden) seems to be crucial for parables, this second standard applies more obviously to action stories, sagas, and creeds.

An expression of faith can be called true, then, if (1) it is consistent with the other facts we recognize; (2) refers adequately; and (3) attributes accurately. This criterion picks up central claims from two philosophical theories of truth, truth as correspondence and truth as coherence.

Consistency

First, we can check an expression of faith to see if it coheres with the other facts we recognize. The most obviously false story is the self-deceptive one. Other problems are more subtle.

Someone with blind trust or blind faith is prone to being deceived or self-deceived. A self-deceived person is irrational in a very particular way—the person is committed strongly to two incompatible claims. For example, "I know my son Tommy beat that girl to death, but he's a good boy." Or, "I know smoking causes lung cancer and emphysema, but I'm going to smoke anyway—it won't hurt me." Or, "I know my girlfriend, Jennie, loves only me even though she's been sleeping with James and Robin, too."

Most instances of self-deception are not so blatant as the quotations above suggest. Most self-deception is far more subtle. We believe in one thing strongly and don't realize that it logically entails a contradiction with something else we believe. Or if we have evidence that our belief is wrong, we fail to see the connection between our belief and such counter-evidence.

Blind faith—believing in "what you know ain't so"—can be a form of self-deception or the result of being deceived by someone you trust. I would argue that at least some fundamentalists may be self-deceived because they hold two incompatible claims. For example, some fundamentalist Christians claim not to *interpret* but just to *read* and *believe* the Bible. They typically take the story of God's creation of the world in the book of Genesis in six days as literally true because they read it there and accept it as God's word. Yet this way of understanding the creation story is inconsistent with the fundamentalist claim that they only read and believe the Bible. In fact, they have used their own reasoning to *interpret* this story as a picture or history of events. Whether the Genesis account of creation is understood as an imaginative myth (in the academic sense) that set up a world that was created good or as a history or a picture or a news report of events is a matter of interpretation.

A book neither interprets nor appraises itself. The Bible cannot say what the Bible means or appraise it as true. Appraisals and interpretations are acts; the Bible is a text or set of texts. We have to do the work of interpreting what it means, and whether God— who can neither deceive nor be deceived in the Christian view— is indeed in some sense speaking to us through it.

To take a particular example, the Bible claims that some 600,000 men (not to mention women and children [Exod 12:37]) left Egypt at the time of the Exodus for Israel, the land that God had promised them, which was then occupied by the Canaanites. But a couple of centuries earlier, an Egyptian ruler had conquered Canaan and much more with an army of 18,000. Had 600,000 men left Egypt in the thirteenth century B.C.E., the Egyptian economy would have collapsed, and there is no record that there was a collapse. Given the military and economic facts, the number of 600,000 men participating in the Exodus from Egypt is inconsistent with other demonstrated facts. Some adjustment is needed to make the story of the Exodus coherent with other facts that we recognize.

The results of scientific and historical investigations are often seen as challenges to faith. Taking them seriously can require folk to change their expressions of faith or to reformulate their reasons for holding their faith claims. Some forms of faith become implausible when those who hold them refuse to take seriously challenges from critical disciplines. As noted earlier, science is not and cannot be a final criterion for assessing the truth of a faith claim, nor is history an ultimate criterion. But to ignore the work of historians or scientists when articulating one's faith is to weaken its credibility. A claim that does not fit with other claims we recognize—including scientific and historical claims—is one that is not justified. But when there is such a clash of claims, "somethin's gotta give" if a belief that expresses our faith is to be justified.

Accuracy of Reference

A second factor is the "accuracy of reference" of a faith claim. Here we utilize the concept of correspondence. To continue with the Exodus account, many scholars think that the Jews who left Egypt may have crossed a marshy area, the Sea of Reeds, rather than the Red Sea (as depicted in DeMille's film *The Ten Commandments*). In this, there is a disagreement about the correct reference in the story regarding the location of the Exodus—and of how we imagine the Exodus to have occurred.

If I call the planet Venus "Alpha Centauri," my reference is inaccurate. I have misidentified the planet. If I call Allah my God and am consumed with a lust for money beyond any other commitment, I have misidentified my god. This is another type of inaccurate reference—we mis-designate that of which we speak.

A more difficult issue usually involves a transcendent actor, a god who acts in our world from beyond our world. Did Moses lead the Exodus from Egypt? Or did God? Was Moses an agent empowered by God, who is really responsible? Or was Moses a powerful leader who led his people to wander around in the desert for forty years? Is the Buddha-essence what produces good among people? Or is it something else? Is the God that Jews, Christians, and Muslims worship the creator and sustainer of the universe? Or is the material universe the "final fact"?

In many instances, resolving disputed questions about transcendent actors is practically impossible. There is no direct evidence to determine whether we fail to see what is really going on or if we are imagining something that just is not there. If "accuracy of reference" were the only criterion for justifying faith, that would be a problem. But we do have other standards to use when we cannot apply this one.

Accuracy of Attribution

Third, the more accurate an expression is in attributing a property or quality to something, the more reasonable it is to call it true. As accuracy of reference centered on naming the right agent, so accuracy of attribution centers on describing an agent, place, event, or thing accurately. To say that it is typically hotter in summer in Phoenix, Arizona than it is in Washington DC is accurate. But to say that it *feels* hotter in Washington than in Phoenix may also be accurate (due to the humidity).

To call the creator and sustainer of the universe "good" seems to fly in the face of the mixed good and evil character of the universe. We noted in Chapter 3 that the Christian myth as summarized in Augustine's *Enchiridion* attributes the ills and evils of the universe not to God, but to the necessary imperfection of creation that led somehow to sin. The humanist finds the source of the universe—if it had any sort of source—indifferent to good and evil. The Buddhist traditions attribute suffering to craving. Which of these accurately attributes the sources of suffering?

Again, the great traditions of faith have expressions that have stood a test of time in part because their claims have some plausibility. Other traditions seem less plausible (at least to me). The Christian Scientist who says that matter and death are mortal illusions and that the Science of Life can free one from death seems implausible (or perhaps I just don't "get" it). To attribute pain and death to matter alone nonetheless seems a misattribution, because we suffer spiritually even if we are not in pain.

Perhaps the gravest misattribution is to believe that some of the gods we (mistakenly) worship can be truly dependable sources of meaning and value—of happiness—in our lives. In the commencement speech referred to in the Introduction, David Foster Wallace made the point most eloquently:

> This, I submit, is the freedom of a real education, of learning how to be well adjusted. You get to consciously decide what has meaning and what doesn't. You get to decide what to worship.
>
> Because here's something else that's weird but true: in the day-to day trenches of adult life, there is actually no such

thing as atheism. There is no such thing as not worshiping.
Everybody worships. The only choice we get is what to
worship. And the compelling reason for maybe choosing
some sort of god or spiritual-type thing to worship—be it JC
or Allah, be it YHWH or the Wiccan Mother Goddess, or the
Four Noble Truths, or some inviolable set of ethical principles—is that pretty much anything else you worship will
eat you alive. If you worship money and things, if they are
where you tap real meaning in life, then you will never have
enough, never feel you have enough. It's the truth. Worship
your body and beauty and sexual allure and you will always
feel ugly. And when time and age start showing, you will die
a million deaths before they finally grieve you. On one level,
we all know this stuff already. It's been codified as myths,
proverbs, clichés, epigrams, parables; the skeleton of every
great story. The whole trick is keeping the truth up front in
daily consciousness.

The petty gods that sometimes each of us, and some of us all the
time, treat as irreducible centers of meaning and sources of value
will fail us. We have misattributed divinity to them. In doing so,
we have, like John Willoughby, sacrificed something far more
meaningful and valuable in order to worship those gods.
    What have we lost? Wallace continues:

And the so-called real world will not discourage you from
operating on your default settings, because the so-called real
world of men and money and power hums merrily along in a
pool of fear and anger and frustration and craving and worship of self. Our own present culture has harnessed these
forces in ways that have yielded extraordinary wealth and
comfort and personal freedom. The freedom to all be lords
of our tiny skull-sized kingdoms, alone at the center of all
creation. This kind of freedom has much to recommend it.
But of course there are all different kinds of freedom, and
the kind that is most precious you will not hear much talk
about much in the great outside world of wanting and
achieving. . . . The really important kind of freedom involves

attention and awareness and discipline, and being able truly to care about other people and to sacrifice for them over and over in myriad petty, unsexy ways every day.

That is real freedom. That is being educated, and understanding how to think. The alternative is unconsciousness, the default setting, the rat race, the constant gnawing sense of having had, and lost, some infinite thing.

Wallace offers no way to choose among the gods worthy of faith, a point to which we will return. He does, however, argue that the finite gods that will be consumed by the passage of time, the twists of fate, or the reality of death are not worth worshiping. Beauty fades with time, power and money are vulnerable to fate, and every nation fades, loses its way, or is defeated in time. These gods have no power over life unless we choose to give it to them, and no power at all to save us from death.

Perhaps John Willoughby (and others who worship finite gods) should have considered Blaise Pascal's wager argument. For Willoughby's loss of love and real meaning shows one of the ways that worship of the finite gods cannot fulfill our real desires, even though they promise to fulfill our immediate desires. These are the gods of the rat race, not of real freedom. Or so Wallace proclaims. To understand what these finite gods really offer requires us to see if the myth that renders them divine is coherent. In short, it seems not: finite gods threaten to eat us alive. It seems inaccurate, and even foolhardy, to attribute power to them to make our lives whole and true; they are not worthy of worship.

In sum, coherence, accuracy of reference, and accuracy of attribution must all be taken into account before we can claim that the beliefs we use to express our faith—and the faith thus expressed in them—are justified. Faith, however, is not merely a matter of belief. It is also a relationship. Hence, we have to ask how the term *true* applies to other aspects of a relationship.

Promoting Authenticity

"Be true to yourself." A faith that fails to enable us to be authentic human beings, authentically "who we are," fails to enable us to be true to ourselves. An expression of faith—a story or claim or practice—can be called true if it is one that enables communities or individuals to be "true to themselves."

Some might find it odd to take authenticity as a criterion for appraising a faith. If expressions of faith were scientific propositions or sagas, such an objection might be reasonable. But faith is a relationship. We do assess the authenticity of relationships. For example, we can ask if the love my beloved and I share really promotes my being true to myself and her being true to herself. Similarly, we can ask if our faith in our god or gods promotes my being true to myself (although I don't see how we can assess such relationships from the gods' side). Assessing faith is assessing a relationship, not merely justifying a proposition.

Authenticity is a slippery concept. To explore it, we can compare John Willoughby and Lorenzo Smythe. I want to say that Smythe was true to himself—despite the challenges to accounting for his personal identity—whereas Willoughby failed to be true to himself. What reasons can I give for that judgment?

First, selves are developed. Whatever my genetic inheritance is, it does not constitute my self. My self emerges over time as a function of what I can do with that inheritance. How I am nurtured, how people respond to me, how I respond to that nurturing process and to other people—these are some of the key components in self development.

The question of being an authentic self is not solved merely by understanding where one began, but by assessing where one is and where one is heading in life. Willoughby was a cad. As Jane Austen portrays him, his devotion to money and pleasure has made him an unhappy man. He does not love Miss Grey, whom he married. He knows what he missed in abandoning Marianne. His god "ate him alive" by making his life—his self—unhappy. Lorenzo, on the other hand, sacrificed his old life. He abandoned Smythe and became Joseph Bonforte. Decades earlier he had begun to head his life in a worthwhile direction, one of service to all peoples. As he looks over the self he has become, he is satisfied—not that he has accomplished everything he wanted to get done, but that he has lived a life worth living. He became an authentic self.

Second, we learn how to become ourselves. It is a process or a journey. Our culture gives us streams of ideals worth living out and of gods to have faith in. We value an ideal or have faith in a god because (a) others teach us by their lives and stories what the significance of those ideals and gods is, and (b) we respond by accepting one or more of those ideals and learning how to value ideals and have faith in one or more of those gods. Moralistic therapeutic deism amalgamates some of those implicit ideals and patterns into the worship of the Cosmic Butler. It may express the faith of some. But if so, it is akin to narcissism. And can a narcissist ever be an authentic self?

Third, what is significant to me is not meaningful because I subjectively give it significance. Rather, I find something that is valued by others and respond positively to it. This is an implication of the insight that faith is not merely a choice but in some sense a gift or happy discovery. When I taught at a major state university, I was told (not only with tongue-in-cheek) that football was the religion and the coach was like god. That was a cultural given. I could accept or reject football as an irreducible center of meaning and source of value. But my choice did not give football its significance. It was a real faith (especially for some alumni) no matter what I thought of it. I could only accept or reject it as my "religion." Conversely, what I could not do was make belching the irreducible source of meaning and center of value in my life. Belching on command might be something I excel at (especially in bars or at parties), but it is at best eccentric to make belching the expression of one's faith and the perfect belch (whatever that might be) the ideal of one's life. The point is that meaning arises not from *my* desiring or devotion to something that is its source, but from *what* I desire or am devoted to. My choice does not make things worthwhile, meaningful, or divine. It is true that something is the source of meaning for *me*. But I do not *make* it meaningful. I *find* it so and *accept* it as such.

Fourth, for a faith to promote authenticity it has to promote the development of an authentic self, a self that is living a life worth living. Wallace argues that devotion to some of the gods of our culture will destroy us. If that is so, is the self developed in the worship of money or pleasure or allure a self worth becoming? If you think so, then you will find that such a devotion truly promotes living an authentic human life. If you do not, then you must find that another form of faith will more truly promote living authentically (unless, of course, authenticity means nothing to you).

The criterion of authenticity, of becoming true to oneself, shows that we find an irreducible center of meaning and source of value and then choose to accept it. Having faith in that god or those gods either leads to a life worth living or it does not. We can discern the difference only by reflection on those individuals whose lives show what it means to worship those gods and whether the sacrifices such worship entails are good sacrifices—hence, the importance of what we called action stories in Chapter 4.

The god of money enmeshes us in the culture of finance; allure places our center in the world of beauty; henotheistic patriotism ("my country, right or wrong") makes us prefer our nation (or its government or political party) and despise, ignore, or sacrifice whatever seems not of benefit to us; secular humanism links us to all the best in all humanity. Which of these faiths promotes developing an authentic human life? Among all the gods proposed for our faith in the multiple currents in our varied culture, which one or ones do I find promote my becoming an authentic self?

Teaching Fidelity

The complement to being true to yourself is being true to others. We may be true to our lovers or we may be unfaithful. We may be true to our ideals or blow with the wind. We may be true to our gods or have little faith. If authenticity is not purely subjective, as argued above, it involves us with others. Because faith is a relationship, authenticity is connected with fidelity. Being true to oneself is connected to being true to others.

We sometimes forget that fidelity and authenticity are closely linked. For example, President John F. Kennedy said: "Ask not what your country can do for you. Ask what you can do for your country." Although his remarks sound as if the first injunction was opposed to the second, I think that reading is inaccurate.

Rather, I'd say he was advocating the right way to begin to find meaning in one's life as a patriot. When asked what one can do for one's country, one will find the country a source of meaning and value (perhaps irreducible, perhaps not).

A community that is faithful to its forbearers, fellow travelers, and future members is a community that carries an authentic tradition. This is one way in which the standard of fidelity applies. Faithful individuals serve as models of exemplary lives in a community. Mother Teresa's commitment to God and to the people she served despite the aridity of her spiritual life is a powerful example of fidelity. She was true to her God, true to herself, and true to others. Indeed, Smythe/Bonforte's service and fidelity to others was what made possible his becoming an authentic self.

Some sorts of life and faith undermine fidelity. Stories of exploitation or of the perversions of justice reveal how some practices that are failures of fidelity can undermine communities. In terms of interpersonal relationships, the most obvious examples are the many stories of adultery that lead to the dissolution of families. Another pattern can be found in the long series of espionage novels of John LeCarré. He explores practices such as double-agency espionage that make any definite sense of fidelity impossible for those who live in and live out the practice. Some of his protagonists (such as Magnus Pym in *The Perfect Spy*) even commit suicide. Learning how to be true to a god and to others may be far more important for being true to oneself than is learning an assemblage of true claims.

It is easy to be true to one's friends or one's country. Some of us are captured by the Peanuts character Linus van Pelt, who said, "I love humanity; it's people I can't stand." The real test of fidelity is not merely how one's faith gets one to deal with one's friends, but rather with those one despises or opposes. Here the ideal of nonviolence is relevant.

We are not violent most of the time. Even those of us who are soldiers or criminals or prize fighters are rarely violent. *Nonviolence* is not this sort of lack of violence. Nor can nonviolence be used to oppress or control others—controlling others requires the willingness to use violence as needed.

Nonviolence has four characteristics. First, the nonviolent person or community is committed to not harming, maiming, or killing another person. Second, the nonviolent person wants to confront the opponent. To let the opponent continue practices that are harmful without resistance is not to deal with the other but to ignore the other. Third, nonviolence is not the same as passivity. Nonviolent people can use demonstrations or strikes or other communal acts of resistance in order to confront the opponent. The purpose is to confront opponents as persons in order to help them to see the evil effects of what they do. Fourth, the ultimate goal of nonviolence cannot be victory over an enemy but the establishment of a community that is peaceful, fair, and just to all its members. Nonviolence requires sacrificing seeking control or domination of others because control and domination are committed to using violence if necessary.

William James recognized the power of nonviolence. He used the term *non-resistance,* but the point is the same. In *The Varieties of Religious Experience* he discussed the power of saintly love:

> Force destroys enemies; and the best that can be said for prudence is that it keeps whatever we already have in safety. But non-resistance, when successful, turns enemies into friends; and charity regenerates its objects.

The point is not to say that a faith that is nonviolent at its heart is the only way to be truly faithful to others. But the practice of nonviolence exemplifies the real test of fidelity: What does the faith, the story, the symbol teach us about our fidelity not only to our friends, but also to our opponents and those we despise?

Perhaps the most humiliating example of the failure of fidelity is the Christian tradition of anti-Semitism, captured in the accusation that the Jews, in executing Jesus, were "Christ-killers." The Gospels say that *some* members who were leaders of the Jewish community in Roman-occupied Palestine may have helped to bring about the execution of Jesus. However, many of his fellow Jews revered Jesus—not the least of whom were his disciples. The Gospels and the Apostles Creed say that he was executed under Pontius Pilate. The obvious fact that the Romans executed Jesus should have made calling Jews "Christ-killers" clearly unacceptable. But if fidelity is measured by how one treats one's opponents and enemies, then the historic anti-Semitism of the Christian tradition provides a good counter-example. Repudiating that conviction and acting to rectify, insofar as possible, the horrible results of anti-Semitism enable Christian communities to be more truly themselves. And it should be noted that most Christian churches have now come to know better; they repudiate anti-Semitism and grieve over their historic failures to be true to all God's children as God is, as the faith they hold teaches them.

The Golden Rule test used to differentiate faiths in Chapter 2 is the real hidden criterion here: To whom is one faithful? How wide or how narrow is the range of one's fidelity? In short, the greater the range of one's fidelity, the more justified is one's faith.

Constancy in Seeking Truth

A faith that creates lives of creative truthfulness can be called true. Those who are true to their ideals live out a faith that can be appraised as more true than individuals who have no ideals or who are opportunists in practice. A faith that promotes the quest for truth, the uncovering of truth, and the telling of truth is a faith that encourages constancy. A true faith has seeking truth as an ideal.

One of the most famous political leaders of the twentieth century was Mohandas K. "Mahatma" Gandhi (1869–1948). He is honored as the Father of the Nation of India. A nonviolent activist in South Africa early in his life and later on in India, the movement he led was a significant factor in ending British colonial rule in India in 1948. His concept of *satyagraha* as the power of truth expresses this criterion for assessing the truth of faith. In a collection of essays, *Non-Violent Resistance*, he wrote:

Satyagraha is literally holding on to Truth, and it means, therefore, Truth-force. Truth is soul or spirit. It is, therefore, known as soul-force. It excludes the use of violence because man is not capable of knowing the absolute truth and, therefore, not competent to punish.

Gandhi described *satyagraha* as involving renunciation, hard work, suffering, and perhaps even death in the service of seeking what is true. He described it as selfless, as concern with self is not primary. He found that a selfless quest for truth meant that one could not wander off the path to truth very long. If one honestly keeps one's eyes on the goal and ignores the difficulties encountered in seeking truth, the search is self-correcting. If one stumbles off the path, the stumbling and difficulties will alert one to return to the right path. A faith that encourages truth seeking and truth telling can be assessed as true.

Some faiths that encourage people to seek *my* truth or *our* truth rather than *the* truth may fit this criterion. But such faiths will not be ranked very high by other standards. The faith that was German Nazism, for example, pursued "our truth" of blood and soil. But even if someone were to find that it encouraged truth seeking, it might not do so well on the standards of coherence, authenticity, and fidelity.

The community of secular humanists who have faith in science also appraises well by this standard. The scientific virtues of honesty, carefulness, and tenacity are an exemplary form of constancy. Scientists seek the truth wherever it may be found. The results of their work are scrutinized by other scientists before they are accepted as true. Moreover, scientists know that they never have the final truth, so they must always continue their quest for truth.

Those who seek what is true are also typically humble. To pursue truth means that one recognizes that one does not have the whole truth. One may be rightly proud of personal accomplishments. One may be satisfied that one has understood and communicated something previously unknown. But this criterion for assessing one's pursuit of truth requires something like the humility expressed in the saying, *The more I learn, the more I realize how little I have learned.*

In Chapter 1 we claimed—in response to Freud—that some faith traditions are self-correcting. A faith that is self-correcting can be seen as meeting the criterion of constancy. Like science, these faiths know that they must always seek what is true because they do not yet have it, at least not in its fullness. Even if we believe that God has revealed eternal and universal truths to humanity, those truths are necessarily expressed in language and other symbols that are temporal and particular. Our concepts cannot be eternal and universal because of historical changes and because the languages in which we express them are not. Hence, a faith tradition is truly constant only if it seeks the truth and is willing to rethink its inheritance in order to express more fully what is true.

CONCLUSION

Appraising the expressions of faith may not be easy. Pastors and other religious leaders do not often encourage it. Of course, fish don't analyze water much either. And for some individuals or communities, assessing faith may be impossible. Some people cannot step out of their faith, even imaginatively, to understand another tradition.

By exploring the standards for appraising expressions of faith, I have sought to show that, however contingent and disputable they may be, appraisals cannot be purely subjective. Appraisals are not arbitrary, capricious, or subject to no standards. Appraisals are always subject to the standards of practices, and good appraisers are people well trained in the practice of appraising. Any fool can give an unwarranted opinion of a claim he knows nothing about. But such opinions are not appraisals in the sense developed here. Just as people unfamiliar with the real-estate market in a neighborhood may have opinions about property values, so can people unfamiliar with religious practices have opinions about religion; such evaluations are of equal weight as those of uninformed real-estate appraisers. Good appraisals of faith require qualified appraisers to make *reliable* claims and to have others accept those appraisals as fair. This is the way appraisals show that claims are true.

Assessing expressions of faith is necessarily contextual. That is, we appraise and assess claims, lives, and stories in a context and for a purpose. Appraisals can change. What has been accepted as a tolerable practice in the past, such as just war and capital punishment, may no longer be appraised as tolerable in the present.

A claim that is accepted as true today might not have been accepted or appraised as true in the past, such as the claim that religious freedom is based in the dignity of the human person created by God—a view rejected by the teaching authority of the Roman Catholic Church in the nineteenth century but then endorsed by the teaching authority of the Roman Catholic Church in the twentieth century. As cultural contexts change and as faith traditions change in response to the contexts in which they are inculturated, appraisals can change. This is a historical fact that I take very seriously.

Contextualism does not imply that all truth is relative. Such a claim is either unobjectionable or empty. If it means that claims are formed in particular times and places and appraisals of them are equally contextual, it is unobjectionable. My shaving mirror, a polished piece of brass, the Hubble telescope, and the tiny mirrors in video projectors, all, if they are well constructed, truly reflect reality in different ways. But all are used for different purposes in different contexts. What we will count as a true reflection will vary in each case. Hence, if one protests against contextualism as developed here as an inappropriate relativism, I ask, "What can the alternative be?" A universal eye, God's point of view, and a mirror for all occasions are inaccessible to us, just as concepts of reality independent of the faiths expressed in myths are unavailable to us humans, even if they can exist. And because the alternative, universal perspective, if one exists, is not within our reach, the objection against the form of contextualism presented here is empty.

Some will also find such a view fragile, unguaranteed by God or the world. But living faith traditions *are* fragile. Faith is risky. To have faith requires having the courage to risk commitment, knowing that it is possible that one's pattern of faith in worship and sacrifice may be wrong. Coping with fragile traditions and risky faith does not require better epistemological foundations, but open-eyed courage tempered with thoughtful reflection on faith and faiths.

Hence, insofar as the religious practices that humans construct and the claims that those practices generate *are* true, the result is that those practices and claims do reflect what there is. The question is, Which faith, and whose practices?

In sum, a faith that enables individuals to live and work in ways that propel them to develop revelatory insight, to utter fitting claims, to be authentically themselves, to keep faith with others, and to keep seeking truth is justifiably appraised as true or "true enough" because it shapes one in a life of truthfulness.

EXCURSUS

Since you've stayed with me this long, I should let you know where I come down. I don't expect you to agree with my views, but I hope that you can use the process I've outlined in this book for better understanding faith.

A decade before Wallace gave his Kenyon College address, I argued in *The Wisdom of Religious Commitment* that narcissistic faith, polytheistic faith, and henotheistic faith did not "grade out" as well as the universalisms do. I agree on the whole with Wallace's view that one should have faith in "some sort of god or spiritual-type thing to worship . . . or some inviolable set of ethical principles" because other finite, "smaller," or more "self-centered" faiths will "eat you alive." They fail the tests of authenticity and fidelity. But I also recognize that each of the monotheistic, monistic, and naturalist types of faith have strengths and weaknesses. Whatever you have faith in, "you bet your life." The project of appraising expressions of faith helps us see where it is wise to place our bets.

Those traditions that make it extremely difficult or impossible to assess faith, whether one's own or those of others, fail the criteria of authenticity, fidelity, and constancy. In my view, they are not really candidates to be assessed as "true" in any robust way. Admittedly, the process of assessing faiths cannot pick out a "sure winner." But it can reduce the number of competitors in the race. Some forms of faith just do not bear up very well under examination and assessment.

Moreover, if one's faith is among the prime candidates, then one probably ought to bet on the faith one has—whatever it is—unless one can no longer accept the assumption that one has faith in the right god. Then one would have a good reason to figure out what one really has faith in as an irreducible source of meaning and center of value.

On the basis of this principle of "if it ain't broke, don't fix it," I remain in the faith tradition in which I was raised: Roman Catholicism. I acknowledge that there are significant difficulties in this tradition. And I recognize that others may assess the situation quite differently. Final fact parity also contributes to the necessity, in my view, of acknowledging such diversity of appraisal as legitimate. Additionally, some of my fellow Catholics might think I'm not as orthodox as they think a good Catholic should be.

I also acknowledge the real attractions of scientific secular humanism. The monotheistic faiths have the problem of accounting for evil in a world that is created good by a good God. My own response to this problem is in my book *The Evils of Theodicy.* I see no actual solution but recognize that a solution may be possible, if not for humans, then for God. On the other hand, scientific secular humanism has the problem of accounting for the evolution of sentient, valuing, loving beings from inanimate matter. There is such a difference between hydrogen and rocks, on the one hand, and humans, on the other, that it is difficult to see how something so simple could spawn something so complex and social. There may be possible solutions to this problem, but I have not seen a convincing actual solution.

I think it unfortunate, but true, that an awful lot of people have faith in gods that will eat them alive. They are sacrificed on the altars of those lesser gods. But all the great universalist traditions offer a spirituality—a pattern of worship and sacrifice—that holds the promise of ultimate hope in some form both for each and for all. And that's another reason I find the faiths carried by the great faith traditions not only possibly true on the whole, but that people live them out in ways that can be assessed very well by all the criteria described here.

Appendix

An Argument about Projection Theories

If you are not persuaded by the "easy answer" to the challenge of projection theories given in Chapter 5, here's a more sophisticated argument using some contemporary work in philosophical theories of knowledge (epistemology) that shows why we ought not accept projection theories.

My first claim is that a fundamental point made by projection theorists is right: we *do* construct our images of the gods. But I also maintain that such construction is characteristic of all human knowing. Hence, the gods we have faith in may be constructed, but so is everything else we make claim to know. So the main point of projection theories is undermined; that is, the gods are not special cases of illusory projection but, as other things people talk of and know, they are examples of a common human practice. Thus, just as we need to assess or appraise everyday sorts of claims, so we need to appraise faith claims.

PROJECTIONS AND CONSTRUCTIONS

Many humanists claim that humans make gods in their own image and likeness (rather than the other way around). They recognize that science is a human creation, too, but they find that science has empirical support. The gods, they claim, do not. So there's a difference, or so some claim. I claim that we do indeed

129

construct our expressions of faith as projection theorists say, but I argue that this does not necessarily imply that the gods of faith must be illusions.

Freud's theory (see Chapter 1) is only one of the projection theories of belief. The German philosopher Ludwig Feuerbach (1804–72) is often named as the originator of such theories. He once argued a form of projection theory somewhat different from Freud's. Rather than finding religious beliefs no more than the irrational product of human wishes, Feuerbach argued that religious beliefs were the imaginative objectifications of human qualities. When we see God as pure love, for example, we are simply projecting on an imaginary being our recognition that love is a profound healing force in our lives. Whether Freudian illusions or Feuerbachian images, projection theories take the gods to be fictions.

There is a truth in projection theories. We humans do construct our images of our gods. We draw our models for the supernatural gods from what we know in this world. We model our talk of God's justice on human justice, and divine love on human love. We also construct our more worldly gods, like power or success, by making these values the irreducible source(s) of meaning and center(s) of value in our lives. These are clearly values in our society. Some of us make them our gods. That we do construct our gods, or at least our images of them, is one good reason that projection theories remain popular.

The problem in projection theories is that all images and ideas we *construct* are not *projections.* Nor are they necessarily irrational illusions rooted in human wishes.

A number of contemporary philosophers have argued in various ways that we construct *whatever* we know. Even if our knowledge is about the real world, the concepts we use and the theories we develop to explain the world are human constructs. *We* named the planet Mars. Mars is our concept; the planet did not name itself.

While there are stars, butterflies, and quarks, the concepts we use to speak of them, "stars" as opposed to planets or anything else, "butterflies," as distinct from moths, hummingbirds, or flying ants, and "quarks" as differentiated from other subatomic participles, are human constructs. Thus, the images of the gods we have faith in may be human constructs, *but so is everything else we think of.*

In these constructivist views the meanings of the images and ideas we use are *contextual*, that is, formed by how those ideas or images are related to the other ideas or images we use to communicate. We learn how to understand these ideas by learning how to use them in practice. We learn how to differentiate jumbo jets from commuter jets, fighters, helicopters, hot-air balloons, and anything else that can be seen by plane spotting. The more differentiations we can make, the more precise our knowledge becomes.

The expressions of faith discussed in Chapters 3 and 4 shape the contours of our faith and provide the context that gives meaning to our symbols of our god or gods. The more we can differentiate the ways we relate to our gods and recognize the similarities and differences between our god or gods and the gods of others, the more precise becomes our understanding of our faith.

Our ideas and images are expressed in terms that get their meanings from the ways we use them and the contexts we use them in. For example, consider *fire.* On any occasion we use the term, it gets its meaning in its context. If I yell it out in a crowded and smoky theater, if I bark it out as a command to a squad of soldiers, if I recognize it as a symbol of the divine, or if I use it to remove a person from a job, the term receives its significance from how I use it in the context. The purposes for which we utter the word or sentence, the circumstances in which we utter it, and the audience to which it is addressed all shape the meaning of the word or sentence. When we examine our language in use, this contextual constructivism makes sense.

The inference to be drawn from the contextual constructivist approach is that whatever claims we express are also constructs. We communicate in linguistic acts—we speak or write. Whatever claims we make are also constructs, because communicating those claims is possible only because we make them using a language. If there were no language, we could make no claims, give no orders, make no promises. We could not talk of stars, butterflies, quarks, or gods. So, if languages are human constructions, then all claims made in them are fundamentally constructed. If all claims are constructed, and if some of them are true, then all true claims are constructed. The question, then, is not so much whether our claims are constructed, but which, if any, of these constructed claims we can call true. If contextual constructivism is on the right track, then this question applies to all claims we make, including claims made about god or gods in expressing our faith.

The Problem of Anti-Realism

An objection to conceptual constructivism arises at this point. If we construct all our claims, are they not in some way unreal or arbitrary? If we construct all we know, then are not the objects of our knowing—from "stars" to "God" to "aluminum" to "maple trees"—mere fabrications or outright fictions? Does conceptual constructivism not imply that all our ideas are like the constellations we "see" in the night sky? In other words, nothing definite is really "there" to make the constellation. So, does that mean that nothing definite is really there to make stars or maple trees or gods or aluminum?

In one version of conceptual constructivism, associated with some postmodern thinkers, our concepts do not, in some sense, match or mirror or reflect reality any more than starry constellations do. However, constructivist accounts of knowledge do not necessarily entail such radical anti-realism.

Strong anti-realism is problematical for many reasons, not the least of which is that it is so strongly counter-intuitive. We may have our doubts about gods and constellations, but we cannot avoid thinking that when we talk about Fido, we mean our real dog Fido; when we talk of Alpha Centauri, we mean a real star; and when I talk of "my daughters," there are two real women of whom I speak. It seems so obvious that whatever I assert about any of them is true if it reflects what there is about them and false if it does not. A thorough anti-realism that rejects this obvious point is not an easy position to hold.

Some anti-realists claim that truth is nothing more than what our peers let us get away with. They would assert that a claim made by an engineer, for example, is "true" if it is well formed in a language that engineers use and is accepted by other engineers. These anti-realists then generalize this point more formally: claims we make are true if competent users of a language accept them as true.

Anti-realists claim that there is no need for a "realistic" theory of truth. A realist theory—one that assumes a claim to be true if the claim matches or mirrors or refers to what there is in the real world—is superfluous. "Look at the way we 'prove' our claims— we convince others that they are true. That's the way truth works. Truth is merely another rhetorical trope, not a privileged standard." So claims the anti-realist.

Many philosophers from ancient times to the present have assumed realism is the foundation of truth. In realism, our knowledge is said to be grounded in the "fact" that our true claims mirror the-world-as-it-is-in-itself (realism) and the "fact" that the-way-the world-is-in-itself is exactly what makes our claim true (foundationalism). My claim that I have two and only two daughters is true because I do have only two daughters. So say the realists. How do anti-realists challenge such an obvious view? An example shows one way of supporting their view.

Consider someone making this claim: "That tree is a sugar maple." The criterion for "that tree is a sugar maple" being true is not the tree that the speaker refers to in uttering the sentence (as a realist might say), but by whether one uses the term "sugar maple" in a way that passes muster with one's interlocutors who have decided to call sugar maples only that few species of the many maples that people actually tap for sap to boil into syrup and sugar. Sugar maples do not exist in the real world independent of our concept of them. Indeed, we literally cannot say what exists in the real world independent of our concepts. How could we conceptualize and communicate what-there-is-independent-of-concepts without concepts of some sort, however vague? A world beyond our concepts is literally inconceivable, incommunicable, unthinkable.

Hence, it is a confusion to say that the world is in any useful way "given" independent of our concepts. Since our concepts are constructed and their uses are given in a constructed linguistic system, "reference-to-things-as-they-are-outside-our-concepts-of-them" is incoherent. It is like trying to talk about what cannot be talked about. Hence, it is useless as a foundation for or a criterion of truth. It is a philosophical delusion to think that right referencing or mirroring whatever there is makes a claim true.

Anti-realism applies just as well to the gods. Just as *sugar maple* is not a thing-in-the-world-independent-of-language, but a concept that people can and do use for certain purposes, so *god* is not a thing-in-the-world-independent-of-language, but a concept that people can use or avoid. *God,* like *sugar maple,* is a human construct, a fabrication, or a fiction according to the anti-realists. Neither the reality nor unreality of *god* or certain trees gives these concepts meaning. Neither the reality nor unreality of *god* or certain trees makes claims using these concepts true or false.

Beyond Anti-Realism

Such a bald sketch may fail to convey the attraction of an anti-realist version of conceptual constructivism. Nonetheless, many philosophers and some theologians have come to accept its basic outline. Yet one does not have to pay the price of anti-realism to get the theoretical benefits and insights of constructivism. Now I want to show how we can (and should) separate constructivism from anti-realism.

Here's the argument. Anti-realists claim that most of us, including philosophers, have been afflicted with a bad assumption, that is, that our ideas, concepts, and claims are true *because* they mirror the "real" world. They then attack the view that reflecting reality is a criterion for the truth of a claim using arguments like those sketched above. But they do not usually consider the possibility that the "mirroring" relationship might not be a *criterion* for judging the truth of a claim, but a *condition* that makes our claims right or an *effect* of our getting our claims right. In other words, accuracy of reference or "mirroring" may indeed be what *makes* the content of claims true, but that fact (if it is a fact) is not something that we can use to *judge* or *assess* whether claims are true or not. What makes a claim true is one thing. How we assess those claims is another. The anti-realist may well be right about the way we *warrant* or *justify* our claims but wrong about *why* those claims are true.

I call a form of realism compatible with contextual constructivism *consequential realism*. Another example will show how consequential realism is different from anti-realism.

I may be able unerringly to pick out sugar maples from other trees in a forest. The skill I have developed to identify sugar maples makes my claim, "This is a sugar maple," reliable. Such a skill in practical forestry is learned by engaging in the practice of sugaring, that is, tapping trees for their sap, collecting it, and boiling it down into syrup. Exercising the skill to identify sugar maples is simply using concepts that we have constructed in the course of horticultural and scientific practices that we learn and call sugaring.

Assume you want to tap all the sugar maples in a grove on your property for their sap so you can make maple syrup. You begin by asking me how many sugar maples are in the grove (so you can figure out how many taps to buy and how much tubing to get to collect the sap into tubs). I take the time to examine the grove and then reply, "There are 237 mature, tappable sugar maples in this grove." This claim is *reliable* only if I have the skill to identify sugar maples and I have exercised that skill, that is, engaged in the practice of identifying sugar maples properly. You will *accept* that the claim is true if I have convinced you that I am an expert on sugar maples and that I have counted them correctly. But what *makes* the claim *true* is the fact (if it is a fact) that there are 237 trees we call sugar maples in the grove that can indeed be tapped.

Notice that this claim cannot be called "true of the world independent of the concept 'sugar maple.'" It is true in our world where we have concepts of sugar maples and property, among others. It is "true of the world as conceptualized to include certain trees we call 'sugar maples.'" This claim is *acceptable* (as true) if those who can recognize tappable sugar maples agree on finding 237 sugar maples in the grove, should they take time to check that claim.

But also notice that there are significant differences between a claim being reliably produced, being true, and being accepted as true. This is the key difference overlooked by those who infer anti-realism is a necessary implication of constructivism. Would you say the claim is false if someone else finds 239 mature sugar maples in the grove? Or 235? Or 517?

Clearly, if one of us finds 517 tappable sugar maples and the other finds 237, one of us (at least) is very unreliable. You shouldn't accept either claim. Such discrepancy is a sign that we really don't know whether either claim is true. At least one of us doesn't know what he or she is doing.

However, if two others skilled in sugaring check the grove, and one finds 235 and the other 239 sugar maples to be tapped, that would be good reason to think that the person who found 517 is unreliable and that my finding 237 was pretty reliable. We may not be able to identify precisely what made the person who counted 517 unreliable, even as we cannot precisely agree on the number of trees to be tapped. That claim is not even "in the running" to be accepted as true (unless some wildly odd circumstances obtain, such as three of us conspiring to deceive the farmer, but we can leave these deviant cases aside here).

But what of those who find 235 or 239? Does that make my claim that there are 237 sugar maples *false*? I think not. The three investigators come out close enough in our counts to suggest that we are reliable in our practice and have exercised it well. Moreover, if the fact that there are XXX sugar maples in the grove makes one of these claims true and the others false, how can we tell? We simply don't have access to "the facts" independent of our constructed concepts and practical investigations. All we can do is count until we get a number or a range of numbers that is good enough to work with. This sort of claim doesn't have to be precisely accurate, just accurate enough for present purposes (whatever those purposes are) to be called true. Mostly, we don't need to quibble about the count being exactly right if the claim is true enough.

FAITH IN THE LIGHT OF CONSTRUCTIVISM

The facts independent of our concepts are not a criterion for the reliability or acceptability of a claim as true: this is the insight of constructivism. "Mirroring states of affairs or things in the world does not constitute a claim's being true": This is the *false* implication many anti-realists draw from constructivism. There is no reason to think that mirroring what-there-is (including what we have constructed) cannot be a *result* of our claim being right; one could say, with appropriate qualifications, that sufficient accuracy of mirroring even *makes the claim true*. But "mirroring" is not a relation independent of our practices, nor is it a foundation for our practices, nor is it a criterion for the truth of our assertions.

Thus, mirroring the world cannot provide a practice-independent criterion of a claim's being true. The error of those we have called foundational realists is to infer from the realist view that mirroring the world or part of it *makes* a claim true, that such mirroring can be used (1) to *show* whether a claim is true or false, or (2) to show whether a claim is *acceptable* as true in a community of inquirers.

Mirroring is neither a criterion for judging whether our claims are true nor a foundation for showing that claims are true. Mirroring is a slippery concept. Given constructivism, we have to acknowledge that mirrors, whether in makeup kits, on walls, in video projectors, or in telescopes simply do not perfectly mirror what there is (and I think they cannot do so, but that's another argument we don't need to develop here).

Constructivists' analyses and arguments have undermined such foundational realism, but a consequential realism is left unscathed. So mirroring what-there-is may be the *result* of our reliably produced claims and may be what makes our claims true, but it is *not a criterion* for judging or showing our claims as true. And, in fact, what makes the claims that there are 235, 237, or 239 sugar maples in the grove "true enough" is that there are about 237±3 trees there that fit our constructed concept of "sugar maple."

The application of this view to assessing faith is clear: Even if we construct our images of God and the gods, and even if the existence of a god or God is what *makes* our faith true, we still need to figure out *which* of our faiths, if any, we can call true. So even if our gods are constructs, that doesn't make them different from anything else we think about. Neither maple trees nor gods are "there" for us to know somehow independent of our concepts of them.

Hence, as we can and do assess claims people make, we can and should assess our faiths. For if we do get our claims "true enough" for the purpose of living a satisfying life, then we may be worshiping the true god or gods as a consequence. We may project the gods as projection theorists say, but if we do, that is just one instance of a common, if not universal, way that humans know—through constructions. To dismiss this one class of projections as illusions either makes everything we know an illusion or singles out one type of projection without sufficient reason. To say they are inconsistent because what is found, shown, or revealed is constructed is simply a confusion; if all our concepts are constructed, then whatever is talked about and conceptualized as found, shown, or revealed is constructed, just like everything else we think. If there is a contradiction, then it afflicts all our concepts, not just our images of our gods.

References

In order to keep distractions in the text to a minimum, I have chosen a referencing method more commonly found in biographies. The brief citations here are to author, date of publication, and pages or standard reference. The sources can be found in the following Works Consulted section, where original dates of publication are included parenthetically when they were available. Many of the texts cited are easily found by an Internet search using authors' names and/or key words.

Page	Initial Words	Citation
1	There are these two young fish . . .	David Foster Wallace (2005)
3	Faith is believing . . .	Mark Twain (1897)
6	Pascal's Wager	Blaise Pascal (1958), 65–69
11	Ivan Karamazov	Fyodor Dostoevsky (1976), 244
11	Matthew Arnold	Matthew Arnold (1970), 27
14	Genuine Option	William James (1897), 11
16	Schleiermacher	F. D. E. Schleiermacher (1928), 12
18	Barth, faith as a gift	Karl Barth (1975), I/2, 706
18	Aquinas, faith as a virtue	Thomas Aquinas (1947–48), I-II, q. 55, a. 1. 17
18	Tillich, ultimate concern	Paul Tillich (1957)

21	Final Fact Parity	Compare Harry V. Stopes-Roe (1977) and Terence Penelhum (1983)
23	Freud responded . . .	Sigmund Freud (1961), 53
28	Habitual center of one's energy . . .	William James (1997), 165
30	Ten thousand difficulties . . .	John Henry Newman (1865), 239
30	No faith without doubt . . .	Paul Tillich (1957), 16–22
32	Treasure is what we value . . .	Nicholas Lash (2008), 21
46	In the years . . .	James Wm. McClendon (1974), 39–64
46	Give me something to die for . . .	Dag Hammarskjöld (1966), 85
60ff.	The Humanist Manifesto	American Humanist Association (2003)
63ff.	*Enchiridion*	Augustine of Hippo (1960)
65ff.	Moralistic Therapeutic Deism	Christian Smith and Melinda L. Denton (2005), 162–63
66	Divine Butler and Cosmic Therapist	Christian Smith and Melinda L. Denton (2005), 165
70	Brief and powerless . . .	Bertrand Russell (1963), 54
70	United with his fellow-men . . .	Bertrand Russell (1963), 53
74	Stories of Faith	Compare John Dominic Crossan (1975) and Terrence W. Tilley (1985)

79   Amid such a [purposeless] world . . . Bertrand Russell (1963), 45

81   Well, I don't know what . . .   Martin Luther King, Jr. (1968)

83   The show must go on . . .   Robert A. Heinlein (1956), 86–87

90   *Darsán*   Diana L. Eck (1998), 3–10

91   These symbols in mathematics . . .   Paul Tillich (1957), 41–43

110   He reflected on the ancient Greek . . . Martin Heidegger (1959), 102–6

113   To take a particular example . . .   Terrence W. Tilley (1985), 150

115f.   This, I submit . . .   David Foster Wallace (2005)

116f.   And the so-called real world . . .   David Foster Wallace (2005)

120   Ask not what your country . . .   John F. Kennedy (1961)

122   Non-violence has four . . .   James Wm. McClendon (1974), 69–70

122   Force destroys enemies . . .   William James (1997), 284

123   Satyagraha . . .   Gandhi (1967), 3

Works Consulted

American Humanist Association. 2003. *The Humanist Manifesto III.* Online at www.americanhumanist.org.

Aquinas, Thomas. 1947–48 (1273). *Summa Theologica.* Translated by the Fathers of the English Dominican Province. New York: Benziger Brothers.

Arnold, Matthew. 1970 (1873). *Literature and Dogma.* Edited and Abridged by James C. Livingston. New York: Frederick Ungar.

Augustine of Hippo. 1960 (421/423). *St. Augustine's Enchiridion or Manual to Laurentius Concerning Faith, Hope and Charity.* Translated by Ernest Evans. London: S.P.C.K.

Austen, Jane. 1996 (1811). *Sense and Sensibility.* New York: Dover Publications.

Barth, Karl. 1975. *Church Dogmatics.* 2d ed. Translated by G. W. Bromiley. Edited by T. F. Torrance and G. W. Bromiley. Edinburgh: T. & T. Clark.

Crossan, John Dominic. 1975. *The Dark Interval: Towards a Theology of Story.* Niles, IL: Argus Communications.

Dostoevsky, Fyodor. 1976 (1880). *The Brothers Karamazov.* The Constance Garnett Translation Revised by Ralph E. Matlaw. New York: W. W. Norton.

Eck, Diana L. 1998. *Darsán: Seeing the Divine Image in India.* 3d edition. New York: Columbia University Press.

Feuerbach, Ludwig. 1881. *The Essence of Christianity.* 2d edition. Translated by Marian Evans. London: Trubner and Co.

Freud, Sigmund. 1961 (1927). *The Future of an Illusion.* Translated by James Strachey. New York: W. W. Norton and Co.

Gandhi, Mohandas K. 1967. *Non-Violent Resistance.* New York: Schocken Books.

Hammarskjöld, Dag. 1966 (1964). *Markings.* Translated by W. H. Auden and Leif Sjöberg. Foreword by W. H. Auden. London: Faber and Faber.

Heidegger, Martin. 1959 (1953). *An Introduction to Metaphysics.* Translated by Ralph Manheim. New Haven, CT: Yale University Press.

Heinlein, Robert A. 1956. *Double Star.* A Signet Book. New York: New American Library.

James, William. 1897. *The Will to Believe and Other Essays in Popular Philosophy.* New York: Longmans Green.

Joyce, James. 2007 (1916). *A Portrait of the Artist as a Young Man: Authoritative Text, Backgrounds and Context, Criticism.* New York: W. W. Norton.

———. 1997 (1902). *The Varieties of Religious Experience: A Study in Human Nature.* A Touchstone Book. Introduction by Reinhold Niebuhr. New York: Simon and Schuster.

Kennedy, John F. 1961. "Inaugural Address." Inaugural Addresses of the Presidents of the United States. Washington DC: U.S. G.P.O., for sale by the Supt. of Docs., U.S. G.P.O., 1989. Online at bartleby.com.

King, Dr. Martin Luther, Jr. 1968. "I've Been to the Mountaintop." Online at www.drmartinlutherkingjr.com,

Lash, Nicholas. 2008. *Theology for Pilgrims.* Notre Dame, IN: University of Notre Dame Press.

McClendon, James Wm., Jr. 1974. *Biography as Theology: How Life Stories Can Remake Today's Theology.* Nashville, TN: Abingdon Press.

Newman, John Henry. 1890 (1865). *Apologia pro Vita Sua.* 2d edition. London: Longmans, Green, and Co.

Niebuhr, H. Richard. 1960. *Radical Monotheism and Western Culture.* New York: Harper and Row.

Pascal, Blaise. 1958 (1670). *Pensées.* Introduction by T. S. Eliot. New York: E. P. Dutton.

Penelhum, Terence. 1983. *God and Skepticism. A Study in Skepticism and Fideism.* Dordrecht and Boston: D. Reidel.

Puzo, Mario. 1969. *The Godfather.* New York: G. P. Putnam's Sons.

Russell, Bertrand. 1963. *Mysticism and Logic and Other Essays.* New York: Doubleday Anchor Book.

Schleiermacher, Friedrich Daniel Ernst. 1928 (1830). *The Christian Faith.* English Translation of the second German edition. Edited by H. R. MacIntosh and J. S. Stewart. Edinburgh: T. & T. Clark.

Smith, Christian, and Melinda Lundquist Denton. 2005. *Soul Searching: The Religious and Spiritual Lives of American Teenagers.* Oxford: Oxford University Press.

Stopes-Roe, Harry V. 1977. "The Intelligibility of the Universe." In *Reason and Religion*, ed. S. C. Brown, 44–71. Ithaca, NY: Cornell University Press.

Taylor, Charles. 1992. *The Ethics of Authenticity*. Cambridge: Harvard University Press.

Tilley, Terrence W. 1985. *Story Theology*. Wilmington, DE: Michael Glazier.

———. 1991. *The Evils of Theodicy*. Washington DC: Georgetown University Press.

———. 1995. *The Wisdom of Religious Commitment*. Washington DC: Georgetown University Press.

Tillich, Paul. 1957. *Dynamics of Faith*. New York: Harper and Row.

Twain, Mark. 1897. *Following the Equator.* Chapter 12 (heading). Online at www.gutenberg.org.

Wallace, David Foster. 2005. "Transcription of the 2005 Kenyon College Commencement Speech–May 21, 2005." Online at www.marginalia.org. Revised and published as *This Is Water: Some Thoughts Delivered on a Significant Occasion, about Living a Compassionate Life*. New York: Little, Brown and Company, 2009.

Weber, Max. 1958 (1904). *The Protestant Ethic and the Spirit of Capitalism*. Translated by Talcott Parsons. Foreword by R. H. Tawney. New York: Charles Scribner's Sons.

Index of Subjects

Index of Subjects

Index of Names